THE
Family Garden
PLANNER

MELISSA K. NORRIS

HARVEST HOUSE PUBLISHERS
EUGENE, OREGON

Cover and interior design by Dugan Design Group
Illustrations copyright © Brigantine Designs/Mighty Deals
Published in association with the literary agency of WordServe Literary Group, Ltd., www.wordserveliterary.com.

The Family Garden Planner

Copyright © 2020 by Melissa K. Norris
Published by Harvest House Publishers
Eugene, Oregon 97408
www.harvesthousepublishers.com

ISBN 978-0-7369-8139-2 (pbk.)

Printed in China

20 21 22 23 24 25 26 27 28 / RDS—DDG / 10 9 8 7 6 5 4 3 2 1

Contents

Introduction

Welcome to *The Family Garden Planner*, your solution to planning and keeping track of every aspect of your garden, including the seed you use, your planting schedule, harvest yields, and all the other details gardeners like us tend to. My goal is to help you produce more food at home with less stress.

As a homesteader and gardener, I used to get frustrated when I missed the summer dates to plant my fall crops (because, hey, life is messy sometimes). I grew tired of not being able to remember which variety of winter squash I planted a few years ago and didn't want to plant again, and which year I last planted my brassicas in an area of the garden.

Little scraps of paper littered my bulletin board, and notes were scattered willy-nilly over three separate calendars. I had scribbled down each summer's harvest amounts, but my record-keeping system didn't help me very much when it came time to plan and plant again. I needed everything in one easy-to-use place so I could save time, make better decisions, and improve my garden year after year. Because honestly, sometimes if you miss a planting window or don't get a handle on an affliction, you don't get another chance until the following year. In fact, you can lose several years when dealing with some diseases in the soil or in fruit trees.

After writing *The Family Garden Plan*, I decided to use that reliable information to create a user-friendly planner that would help me plan my garden, keep up on the work, and record important information so I could reduce my frustration and enjoy a better garden and more food production every year. I also knew I wasn't the only gardener and homesteader who needed this. Life is busy, and though gardening at its core is simple, it's not always easy to remember all those dates and how well crops produced from year to year.

I also wanted to keep track of our expenses and yields. I was pretty sure our garden was saving us money, but I wanted a better idea of just how much.

This handy tool includes everything you need

to plan your garden, execute your plan, record your results, and have fun with the process—after all, gardening should bring you joy. You can refer back to it year after year because you and I, my friends, we are lifelong gardeners, and Lord willing, we have many decades to fill with growing our own food.

You ready? Let's do this!

How to Get the Most from Your Planner

To get started, work through the charts and worksheets in part 1 to identify which gardening zone you are in, which crops you would like to grow, how much of each crop you'll need to plant, and so on. These worksheets and charts are loaded with helpful information that will help you create the garden that is just right for you.

Next, look in part 3, "Monthly Gardening Tasks by Zone," to find tons of important information about your gardening zone.

Finally, using the plan you created in part 1 and the information you gleaned in part 3, turn back to part 2 and fill out your yearly, monthly, and weekly gardening calendars. The more consistently you use these personalized calendars to plan your garden, schedule your tasks, and record your data, the better your results will be. This data will help you continually improve your garden and make the best decisions for your plants. Each year's garden can be even better than the one before!

Keep your planner where you'll see it daily—by your computer, at your desk, or where you have your morning coffee or tea. The more you use it, the more you'll enjoy it and benefit from having a well-thought-out plan and workable schedule for creating your best garden ever.

PART ONE

Charts and Worksheets

FOOD NEEDS FOR A YEAR

Here is a worksheet to help you document and plan out approximate yearly needs based on your family's eating habits. This will help you during the growing season for fresh eating per week and also with your food preservation for the pantry shelf.

Individual Fruits/Vegetables

Food	Serving Amount Per Meal	Week 1	Week 2	Week 3	Week 4	Weekly Average	Yearly Need
	2 cups, 1 pound, etc.	Serving amount x meals	Serving amount x meals	Serving amount x meals	Serving amount x meals	Total serving amounts divided by 4 weeks	Average weekly use x 52 weeks
green beans	2 cups	2x2 = 4 cups	2x0 = 0 cups	2x1 = 2 cups	2x0 = 0 cups	6 cups/ 4 weeks = 1 1/2 cups	1 1/2 cups x 52 weeks = 78 cups

Combination Recipes

Food	Serving Amount Per Meal	Week 1	Week 2	Week 3	Week 4	Weekly Average	Yearly Need
salsa	1 cup	1x1= 1 cup	1x0= 0 cups	1x1= 1 cup	1x2= 2 cups	4 cups/ 4 weeks= 1 cup	1 cup x 52 weeks = 52 cups

GARDENING ZONES

Determining your gardening zone will help you know which plants will grow and thrive in your area and when to start your seeds indoors, move plants outside, or sow directly into your garden. To discover your gardening zone, simply type your zip code and the words "garden zone," "first frost," and "last frost" into your search bar. Or visit the USDA Plant Hardiness Zone Map at https://planthardiness.ars.usda.gov/PHZMWeb/. It divides North America into zones based on the average annual minimum temperature.

If you can, ask a few experienced gardeners in your area about their planting dates as well. You might even be able to find a local gardening group online—a potential gold mine of information, allowing for more accuracy and planting success.

My gardening zone is _____ .

My average last frost date is _____ .

My average first frost date is _____ .

CROP PLANNING

Now that you know which foods your family is eating a lot of, it's time to decide which of these crops you'll be planting in your garden this year.

When deciding what plants to grow, consider your growing season and what grows easily in your area.

Annual Vegetables	Perennial Vegetables	Fruit	Herbs
zucchini	asparagus	raspberries	rosemary

HOW MUCH TO PLANT

Below you'll find a chart with recommendations for how much to plant per person for a year's worth of food and how much each plant produces on average. Keep in mind, these averages are based on good soil and may differ year to year. I find my tomatoes and beans produce much more than the average listed. Your actual yield will be affected by soil nutrition, weather, and pest conditions.

Bushel	Peck	Quart	Pint
4 pecks 8 gallons 32 quarts 64 pints 128 cups	8 quarts 16 pints 32 cups	2 pints 4 cups	2 cups

How Much Fruit to Plant

FRUIT	Plants per Person	Average Yield Per Plant
Apples		Dwarf: 5–6 bushels Semi-Dwarf: 10–15 bushels Standard: 5–20 bushels
Apricots		Miniature: 1–2 pecks Dwarf: 1–2 bushels Standard: 3–4 bushels
Blackberries	2–4 plants per person	35–70 cups per plant
Blueberries	2 plants per person	15–45 cups depending on maturity of plant
Cherries		**Sweet** Dwarf: 8–10 gallons Semi-Dwarf: 10–15 gallons Standard: 15–20 gallons **Sour** Dwarf: 3–5 gallons Semi-Dwarf: 12–18 gallons

FRUIT	Plants per Person	Average Yield Per Plant
Elderberries	1 plant per person	30-36 cups per mature plant
Grapes	1 vine per person	10-30 cups per vine
Nectarines		Miniature: 1-2 pecks Dwarf: 3-4 bushels Standard: 6-10 bushels
Peaches		Miniature: 1-2 pecks Dwarf: 3-4 bushels Standard: 6-10 bushels
Pears		Dwarf: 6-8 bushels Standard: 12-15 bushels
Plums		**European** Dwarf: 1-1½ bushels Standard: 1-2 bushels **Japanese** Dwarf: 3-4 bushels Semi-Dwarf: 4-5 bushels Standard: 5-6 bushels
Raspberries	10-25 plants per person	1-2 quarts per plant
Rhubarb	2-3 crowns per person	6 cups per crown
Strawberries	20-25 plants per person	1 pound or 1 pint per plant

How Many Vegetables to Plant

VEGETABLES	Average Plants per Person	Average Pounds per Plant	Average Cups per Plant
Asparagus	10–15 per person average	2–3 pounds per plant	4–6 cups
Beans, Dry	15 plants per person	¼ –½ pound per plant	2 cups
Beans, Snap	Bush: 15–20 plants per person Pole: 10–15 plants per person	½ pound per plant ½ pound per plant	Bush: 2 cups Pole: 3–4 cups
Beets	36–40 per person	¼ pound per beet	½ –¾ cup
Broccoli	3–5 plants per person	1 pound per plant	5–6 cups
Brussels Sprouts	2–3 plants per person	¾–1 pound per plant	4 cups
Cabbage (finely chopped/shredded)	3–5 plants per person	2–4 pounds per plant	8–16 cups
Carrots	25–30 per person	¼ pound per carrot	¼ cup
Cauliflower	2–3 plants per person	2 pounds per plant	3–4 cups

VEGETABLES	Average Plants per Person	Average Pounds per Plant	Average Cups per Plant
Celery	3–5 per person	½ pound per plant	2 cups
Corn (Sweet, in husk)	15 plants per person	2 ears per plant	1½ cups
Cucumbers (3–5" pickling cukes)	2–4 plants per person	3–5 pounds per plant	8–15 cups (3–5 quarts whole)
Eggplant	1–2 plants per person	8–10 pounds per plant	32–40 cups
Garlic	15 bulbs per person		
Kale	5 plants per person	1 pound per plant	3–6 cups
Leeks	12–15 plants per person	¼ pound per plant	½ cup
Lettuce	5–10 per person	¼–1 pound per plant	4–6 cups
Okra	6–8 plants per person	1 pound per plant	1½ cups
Onions, storage	15 bulbs per person	½ pound	1 cup
Parsnip	10–12 per person	⅓ pound per plant	⅔ cup

VEGETABLES	Average Plants per Person	Average Pounds per Plant	Average Cups per Plant
Peas, field	30 plants per person	⅛–¼ pound per plant	¼ cup
Peppers	Hot: 1–2 plants per person Sweet: 3–4 plants per person	1–4 pounds per plant	3–10 cups
Potatoes	10–15 plants per person	2 pounds per plant	4 cups
Pumpkins	1–2 plants per person	4–10 pounds per plant	16–40 cups, cubed
Rutabagas	5–10 plants per person	1–3 pounds per plant	11/2–5 cups
Spinach	15 plants per person	¼ pound per plant	1½ cups
Squash, summer (pattypan, yellow, zucchini)	1–2 plants per person	5–20 pounds per plant	12–50 cups
Squash, winter (Hubbard, banana, acorn, butternut, buttercup)	1–2 plants per person	10–15 pounds per plant	10–15 cups
Sweet Potatoes	5 plants per person	2 pounds per plant	5 cups
Tomatoes	5 plants per person	5–15 pounds per plant	7½ cups–22½ cups
Turnips	5–10 plants per person	½ pound per plant	2 cups

CROPS FOR A YEAR

Look at the crops you identified in your Food Needs for a Year section beginning on page 8 and transfer them to the worksheet that follows. Use the How Much to Plant section beginning on page 11 to determine the amount you'll need to reach the desired annual yield for your family.

Individual Fruits/Vegetables

Crop	Desired Annual Yield	Number of Plants Needed (use average cups per plant from the How Many Fruits/Vegetables to Plant)
green beans	39 pints (78 cups)	38 to 40 pole bean plants

Combination Recipes

Crop	Desired Annual Yield	Number of Plants Needed (use average cups per plant from the How Many Fruits/Vegetables to Plant)
tomatoes, salsa	40 cups (for 26 pints of salsa)	3 to 5 plants
onion, salsa	20 cups	20 plants
bell pepper, salsa	20 cups	4 to 6 plants
jalapeno, salsa	4 cups	1 to 2 plants
garlic, salsa	20 cloves	4 to 5 plants

SEED STARTING AND PLANTING

Below is the seed starting and planting chart I use. You won't find all vegetables listed because some plants don't do well started indoors or don't warrant the work for only a few days earlier harvest.

Plant	Start Indoors	Germination Period	Direct Sow (spring and fall dates if applicable for fall crops)	My Sow Date My last frost date_____ My first frost date _____
Basil	4–8 weeks, plant outside 2–3 weeks after last frost	5–10 days	2–4 weeks after last frost	
Beans— bush, pole, and shelled	You can start indoors on the last frost date, but beans don't like their roots messed with, and I prefer to direct sow	6–18 days	3–4 weeks after last frost	
Beets	3 weeks before last frost, plant outside on last frost date	5–21 days	2–4 weeks before last frost and sow up to 8 weeks before first frost in fall	
Broccoli	7 weeks before last frost, plant outside 2 weeks before last frost	4–20 days	2 weeks before last frost, 10–12 weeks before first frost in fall	
Brussels Sprouts	2–3 weeks before last frost, plant outside 2 weeks after last frost	5–15 days	2 weeks after last frost, can direct sow 10 weeks before first frost in fall	
Cabbage	6 weeks before last frost, plant outside 2 weeks before last frost	4–20 days	2 weeks before last frost, 6-8 weeks before first frost in fall	
Carrots		7–21 days	2–4 weeks before last frost, 8-12 weeks before first frost in fall	
Cauliflower	8–10 weeks before last frost, plant outside 4 weeks before last frost Fall crop start 12–14 weeks before first frost, plant outside 8 weeks before first fall frost	4–10 days	2 weeks before last frost	
Chard	4 weeks before last frost, plant outside on last frost date	5–21 days	Last frost date, 10–12 weeks before first frost date in fall	

Plant	Start Indoors	Germination Period	Direct Sow (spring and fall dates if applicable for fall crops)	My Sow Date My last frost date_____ My first frost date _____
Cilantro/ Coriander	4–8 weeks before last frost, plant outside right at last frost	5–10 days	2 weeks before last frost, 6–8 weeks before first frost in fall	
Corn	Best direct sown	3–10 days	2 weeks after last frost	
Cucumber (see Summer Squash)				
Dill	Best direct sown	2–3 weeks	4 weeks after last frost or when soil temp is 60 degrees Fahrenheit or warmer	
Garlic			Plant cloves in ground between 2 weeks before and 2 weeks after first frost in fall for summer harvest. In mild winter climates, plant bulbs 8–10 weeks before last frost in spring for late summer harvest if ground isn't frozen.	
Kale	3–6 weeks before last frost, plant outdoors 2–3 weeks before last frost	4–9 days	2–4 weeks before last frost, 6–8 weeks before first frost in fall	
Lettuce	6–8 weeks before last frost, plant outdoors 3–4 weeks before last frost	2–15 days	2–4 weeks before last frost and 6–8 weeks before first frost in fall	
Marjoram	2–3 weeks; plant outside after all danger of frost has passed	8–10 weeks	1 week after last frost	
Melon	Last frost date, plant outdoors 4 weeks after last frost	4–10 days	4 weeks after last frost	
Okra	4-6 weeks before last frost, plant outside 4 weeks after last frost	5–12 days	4 weeks after last frost	
Onion	10–16 weeks before last frost	7–28 days	bulbs 6 weeks before or 4 weeks after last frost	

Plant	Start Indoors	Germination Period	Direct Sow (spring and fall dates if applicable for fall crops)	My Sow Date My last frost date_____ My first frost date_____
Parsnip		10–21 days	2 weeks before last frost through 12 weeks before first frost in fall	
Pea	8 weeks before last frost, plant outside 4 weeks before last frost	6–17 days	4–6 weeks before last frost through 12 weeks before first frost in fall	
Pepper	4–8 weeks before last frost (in cooler climates I recommend 8 weeks)	Hot, 14–28 days Sweet, 7–14 days	Put seedlings out 3–4 weeks after last frost	
Potato			2- 4 weeks before last frost in spring	
Radish		3–10 days	2–4 weeks before last frost in spring through 8 weeks before first frost in fall	
Spinach	6-8 weeks before last frost, plant outside 4 weeks before last frost	5–21 days	6 weeks before last frost in spring through 6 weeks before first frost in fall	
Squash, Summer and Winter	2 weeks before last frost	3–10 days	2–4 weeks after last frost	
Summer Savory	6–8 weeks; plant outdoors after all danger of frost has passed	2–3 weeks	1 week after last frost	
Sweet Potato			3–4 weeks after last frost in spring	
Tomato	2–8 weeks before last frost (8–10 weeks for cold climates)	5–14 days		
Turnip		5–10 days	2–4 weeks before last frost, 4 weeks before first frost in fall	

CROP ROTATION

Rotate your crops to maintain nutrients in the soil and to avoid disease. If possible, plan for at least a three-year rotation before planting a member of the same crop family in the same place, especially with brassicas and any crop in the *Solanaceae* family. Crop rotation works best when you regularly test your soil and amend it as needed. Here are the four plant types to consider when planning your crop rotation. You can follow this rotation at each planting (if you're doing fall, spring, and summer crops) or year by year.

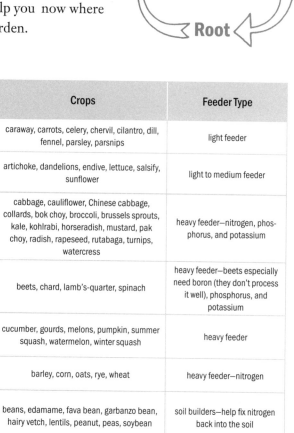

Below is a chart for each crop to help you now where it should fall in this rotation in your garden.

Plant Family Name	Crop Rotation Type	Crops	Feeder Type
Apiaceae (*Umbelliferae*; carrot family)	Root	caraway, carrots, celery, chervil, cilantro, dill, fennel, parsley, parsnips	light feeder
Asteraceae (*Compositae*, daisy family, lettuce family)	Leaf	artichoke, dandelions, endive, lettuce, salsify, sunflower	light to medium feeder
Brassicaceae (*Cruciferae*; brassicas, cole crops, cruciferous crops, mustard family)	Leaf	cabbage, cauliflower, Chinese cabbage, collards, bok choy, broccoli, brussels sprouts, kale, kohlrabi, horseradish, mustard, pak choy, radish, rapeseed, rutabaga, turnips, watercress	heavy feeder—nitrogen, phosphorus, and potassium
Chenopodiaceae (goosefoot family, *beta vulgaris*; beet family)	Root	beets, chard, lamb's-quarter, spinach	heavy feeder—beets especially need boron (they don't process it well), phosphorus, and potassium
Cucurbitaceae (*Cucurbits*; cucumber family, squash family)	Fruit	cucumber, gourds, melons, pumpkin, summer squash, watermelon, winter squash	heavy feeder
Graminae (grains, grass)	Leaf	barley, corn, oats, rye, wheat	heavy feeder—nitrogen
Fabaceae (*Leguminosae*, leguminous crops, legumes; bean, pea or legume family)	Legume	beans, edamame, fava bean, garbanzo bean, hairy vetch, lentils, peanut, peas, soybean	soil builders—help fix nitrogen back into the soil
Liliaceae (lily family; alliums for members of the Allium genus)	Root	asparagus, chives, garlic, leeks, onions, shallots	light feeder
Solanaceae (Solanaceous crops; potato, tomato, or nightshade family)	Fruit	eggplant, peppers (bell and chili), potatoes, tomatillo, tomatoes	heavy feeder

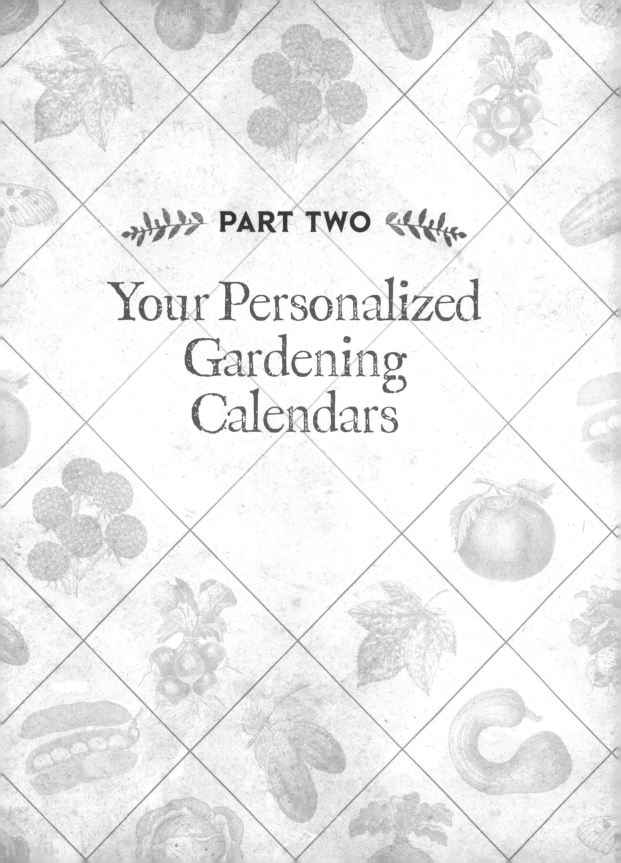

PART TWO

Your Personalized
Gardening
Calendars

N ow that you have used the charts and worksheets in part 1 to create your personalized garden plan, read the important information about your gardening zone in part 3. Then you'll be ready to create your own personalized gardening calendars. You'll find plenty of space to track and record data that's important to you.

Yearly Planning

This section will help you plan out your year at a glance. Here are some items to include:

- predicted and actual first and last frost dates (see Gardening Zones on page 10)
- unusual weather patterns
- planting, germination, first blossom, and first harvest dates of each vegetable type (see Vegetable Performance for a Garden Year on page 28)
- full bloom and first harvest dates for fruit trees and bushes (see Fruit and Orchard Performance for a Garden Year on page 32)
- any large projects (such as installing a new garden bed) that pertain to your food production

In addition, use these pages to record things as they happen in the garden. I find it easiest to record daily things in the weekly sheets and then transfer the most important information onto the Year at a Glance pages so I have an easy-to-review summary of my garden year.

Monthly Planning

Use these pages to record the information you learn in part 3, "Monthly Gardening Tasks by Zone," to make sure you don't miss any planting, harvesting, or other gardening tasks for the crops you wish to put in this year. I've also included an expense tracking sheet for each month. This is especially handy for tax reporting (if you are self-employed or your garden produces some of your income) and budgeting.

Weekly Planning

Finally, use these pages to create your to-do lists for each week and to make any other notes about your garden, including…

- soil tests, soil amendments, and fertilizer application
- appearance of diseases or pests and treatments
- varieties of fruits or vegetables that performed particularly well or poorly
- daily and weekly harvest yields
- direct sow and transplanting dates

Happy gardening!

YEAR AT A GLANCE

January	February

March	April

May	June

July	August

September	October

November	December

VEGETABLE PERFORMANCE FOR A GARDEN YEAR

Plant and Variety	Date Planted	Number of Plants	Days to Germinate	Days to Harvest	First Harvest	Yield Per Plant	Plant Again?
Cucumber: Chicago Pickling	May 1	5	7	55		8+ cups	9 plants

Notes

Check for downy mildew early in the season and prune out larger leaves at base.

Plant and Variety	Date Planted	Number of Plants	Days to Germinate	Days to Harvest	First Harvest	Yield Per Plant	Plant Again?

FRUIT AND ORCHARD PERFORMANCE FOR A GARDEN YEAR

Fruit and Variety	Plant Age	First Bloom	Fruit Harvest	Harvest/Yield
Apple: Honey Crisp	3 Years	May 1	Sept. 2	3 apples

Notes

9 plants

FRUIT AND ORCHARD PERFORMANCE FOR A GARDEN YEAR (continued)

Fruit and Variety	Plant Age	First Bloom	Fruit Harvest	Harvest/Yield

Notes

MONTH AT A GLANCE FOR _____

Sunday	Monday	Tuesday	Wednesday

Thursday	Friday	Saturday	Notes

MONTHLY PLANNING FOR _____

(See part 3, "Monthly Gardening Tasks by Zone")

Garden Tasks for the Month

Must-Do Projects

Notes

MONTHLY EXPENSES

Date	Paid to	Item	Amt.	Yield (if applicable)

 **WEEK AT A GLANCE FOR** _____

	Sunday	Monday	Tuesday	Wednesday
6 a.m.				
7 a.m.				
8 a.m.				
9 a.m.				
10 a.m.				
11 a.m.				
12 p.m.				
1 p.m.				
2 p.m.				
3 p.m.				
4 p.m.				
5 p.m.				
6 p.m.				
7 p.m.				
Weather: High Temp: Low Temp:				
Harvest Yield				

WEEK AT A GLANCE FOR _____

	Thursday	Friday	Saturday	Notes
6 a.m.				
7 a.m.				
8 a.m.				
9 a.m.				
10 a.m.				
11 a.m.				
12 p.m.				
1 p.m.				
2 p.m.				
3 p.m.				
4 p.m.				
5 p.m.				
6 p.m.				
7 p.m.				
Weather: High Temp: Low Temp:				
Harvest Yield				

 # WEEK AT A GLANCE FOR _____

	Sunday	Monday	Tuesday	Wednesday
6 a.m.				
7 a.m.				
8 a.m.				
9 a.m.				
10 a.m.				
11 a.m.				
12 p.m.				
1 p.m.				
2 p.m.				
3 p.m.				
4 p.m.				
5 p.m.				
6 p.m.				
7 p.m.				
Weather: High Temp: Low Temp:				
Harvest Yield				

WEEK AT A GLANCE FOR _____

	Thursday	Friday	Saturday	Notes
6 a.m.				
7 a.m.				
8 a.m.				
9 a.m.				
10 a.m.				
11 a.m.				
12 p.m.				
1 p.m.				
2 p.m.				
3 p.m.				
4 p.m.				
5 p.m.				
6 p.m.				
7 p.m.				
Weather: High Temp: Low Temp:				
Harvest Yield				

WEEK AT A GLANCE FOR _____

	Sunday	Monday	Tuesday	Wednesday
6 a.m.				
7 a.m.				
8 a.m.				
9 a.m.				
10 a.m.				
11 a.m.				
12 p.m.				
1 p.m.				
2 p.m.				
3 p.m.				
4 p.m.				
5 p.m.				
6 p.m.				
7 p.m.				
Weather: High Temp: Low Temp:				
Harvest Yield				

WEEK AT A GLANCE FOR _____

	Thursday	Friday	Saturday	Notes
6 a.m.				
7 a.m.				
8 a.m.				
9 a.m.				
10 a.m.				
11 a.m.				
12 p.m.				
1 p.m.				
2 p.m.				
3 p.m.				
4 p.m.				
5 p.m.				
6 p.m.				
7 p.m.				
Weather: High Temp: Low Temp:				
Harvest Yield				

WEEK AT A GLANCE FOR _____

	Sunday	Monday	Tuesday	Wednesday
6 a.m.				
7 a.m.				
8 a.m.				
9 a.m.				
10 a.m.				
11 a.m.				
12 p.m.				
1 p.m.				
2 p.m.				
3 p.m.				
4 p.m.				
5 p.m.				
6 p.m.				
7 p.m.				
Weather: High Temp: Low Temp:				
Harvest Yield				

WEEK AT A GLANCE FOR _____

	Thursday	Friday	Saturday	Notes
6 a.m.				
7 a.m.				
8 a.m.				
9 a.m.				
10 a.m.				
11 a.m.				
12 p.m.				
1 p.m.				
2 p.m.				
3 p.m.				
4 p.m.				
5 p.m.				
6 p.m.				
7 p.m.				
Weather: High Temp: Low Temp:				
Harvest Yield				

 **WEEK AT A GLANCE FOR** _____

	Sunday	Monday	Tuesday	Wednesday
6 a.m.				
7 a.m.				
8 a.m.				
9 a.m.				
10 a.m.				
11 a.m.				
12 p.m.				
1 p.m.				
2 p.m.				
3 p.m.				
4 p.m.				
5 p.m.				
6 p.m.				
7 p.m.				
Weather: High Temp: Low Temp:				
Harvest Yield				

WEEK AT A GLANCE FOR _____

	Thursday	Friday	Saturday	Notes
6 a.m.				
7 a.m.				
8 a.m.				
9 a.m.				
10 a.m.				
11 a.m.				
12 p.m.				
1 p.m.				
2 p.m.				
3 p.m.				
4 p.m.				
5 p.m.				
6 p.m.				
7 p.m.				
Weather: High Temp: Low Temp:				
Harvest Yield				

MONTH AT A GLANCE FOR _____

Sunday	Monday	Tuesday	Wednesday

Thursday	Friday	Saturday	Notes

MONTHLY PLANNING FOR _____

(See part 3, "Monthly Gardening Tasks by Zone")

Garden Tasks for the Month

Must-Do Projects

Notes

MONTHLY EXPENSES

Date	Paid to	Item	Amt.	Yield (if applicable)

WEEK AT A GLANCE FOR _____

	Sunday	Monday	Tuesday	Wednesday
6 a.m.				
7 a.m.				
8 a.m.				
9 a.m.				
10 a.m.				
11 a.m.				
12 p.m.				
1 p.m.				
2 p.m.				
3 p.m.				
4 p.m.				
5 p.m.				
6 p.m.				
7 p.m.				
Weather: High Temp: Low Temp:				
Harvest Yield				

 **WEEK AT A GLANCE FOR** _____

	Thursday	Friday	Saturday	Notes
6 a.m.				
7 a.m.				
8 a.m.				
9 a.m.				
10 a.m.				
11 a.m.				
12 p.m.				
1 p.m.				
2 p.m.				
3 p.m.				
4 p.m.				
5 p.m.				
6 p.m.				
7 p.m.				
Weather: High Temp: Low Temp:				
Harvest Yield				

 **WEEK AT A GLANCE FOR** _____

	Sunday	Monday	Tuesday	Wednesday
6 a.m.				
7 a.m.				
8 a.m.				
9 a.m.				
10 a.m.				
11 a.m.				
12 p.m.				
1 p.m.				
2 p.m.				
3 p.m.				
4 p.m.				
5 p.m.				
6 p.m.				
7 p.m.				
Weather: High Temp: Low Temp:				
Harvest Yield				

 **WEEK AT A GLANCE FOR** _____

	Thursday	Friday	Saturday	Notes
6 a.m.				
7 a.m.				
8 a.m.				
9 a.m.				
10 a.m.				
11 a.m.				
12 p.m.				
1 p.m.				
2 p.m.				
3 p.m.				
4 p.m.				
5 p.m.				
6 p.m.				
7 p.m.				
Weather: High Temp: Low Temp:				
Harvest Yield				

 # WEEK AT A GLANCE FOR _____

	Sunday	Monday	Tuesday	Wednesday
6 a.m.				
7 a.m.				
8 a.m.				
9 a.m.				
10 a.m.				
11 a.m.				
12 p.m.				
1 p.m.				
2 p.m.				
3 p.m.				
4 p.m.				
5 p.m.				
6 p.m.				
7 p.m.				
Weather: High Temp: Low Temp:				
Harvest Yield				

WEEK AT A GLANCE FOR _____

	Thursday	Friday	Saturday	Notes
6 a.m.				
7 a.m.				
8 a.m.				
9 a.m.				
10 a.m.				
11 a.m.				
12 p.m.				
1 p.m.				
2 p.m.				
3 p.m.				
4 p.m.				
5 p.m.				
6 p.m.				
7 p.m.				
Weather: High Temp: Low Temp:				
Harvest Yield				

 **WEEK AT A GLANCE FOR** _____

	Sunday	Monday	Tuesday	Wednesday
6 a.m.				
7 a.m.				
8 a.m.				
9 a.m.				
10 a.m.				
11 a.m.				
12 p.m.				
1 p.m.				
2 p.m.				
3 p.m.				
4 p.m.				
5 p.m.				
6 p.m.				
7 p.m.				
Weather: High Temp: Low Temp:				
Harvest Yield				

WEEK AT A GLANCE FOR _____

	Thursday	Friday	Saturday	Notes
6 a.m.				
7 a.m.				
8 a.m.				
9 a.m.				
10 a.m.				
11 a.m.				
12 p.m.				
1 p.m.				
2 p.m.				
3 p.m.				
4 p.m.				
5 p.m.				
6 p.m.				
7 p.m.				
Weather: High Temp: Low Temp:				
Harvest Yield				

 # WEEK AT A GLANCE FOR _____

	Sunday	Monday	Tuesday	Wednesday
6 a.m.				
7 a.m.				
8 a.m.				
9 a.m.				
10 a.m.				
11 a.m.				
12 p.m.				
1 p.m.				
2 p.m.				
3 p.m.				
4 p.m.				
5 p.m.				
6 p.m.				
7 p.m.				
Weather: High Temp: Low Temp:				
Harvest Yield				

WEEK AT A GLANCE FOR _____

	Thursday	Friday	Saturday	Notes
6 a.m.				
7 a.m.				
8 a.m.				
9 a.m.				
10 a.m.				
11 a.m.				
12 p.m.				
1 p.m.				
2 p.m.				
3 p.m.				
4 p.m.				
5 p.m.				
6 p.m.				
7 p.m.				
Weather: High Temp: Low Temp:				
Harvest Yield				

MONTH AT A GLANCE FOR _____

Sunday	Monday	Tuesday	Wednesday

Thursday	Friday	Saturday	Notes

MONTHLY PLANNING FOR _____

(See part 3, "Monthly Gardening Tasks by Zone")

Garden Tasks for the Month

Must-Do Projects

Notes

MONTHLY EXPENSES

Date	Paid to	Item	Amt.	Yield (if applicable)

 **WEEK AT A GLANCE FOR** _____

	Sunday	Monday	Tuesday	Wednesday
6 a.m.				
7 a.m.				
8 a.m.				
9 a.m.				
10 a.m.				
11 a.m.				
12 p.m.				
1 p.m.				
2 p.m.				
3 p.m.				
4 p.m.				
5 p.m.				
6 p.m.				
7 p.m.				
Weather: High Temp: Low Temp:				
Harvest Yield				

WEEK AT A GLANCE FOR _____

	Thursday	Friday	Saturday	Notes
6 a.m.				
7 a.m.				
8 a.m.				
9 a.m.				
10 a.m.				
11 a.m.				
12 p.m.				
1 p.m.				
2 p.m.				
3 p.m.				
4 p.m.				
5 p.m.				
6 p.m.				
7 p.m.				
Weather: High Temp: Low Temp:				
Harvest Yield				

 **WEEK AT A GLANCE FOR** _____

	Sunday	Monday	Tuesday	Wednesday
6 a.m.				
7 a.m.				
8 a.m.				
9 a.m.				
10 a.m.				
11 a.m.				
12 p.m.				
1 p.m.				
2 p.m.				
3 p.m.				
4 p.m.				
5 p.m.				
6 p.m.				
7 p.m.				
Weather: High Temp: Low Temp:				
Harvest Yield				

WEEK AT A GLANCE FOR _____

	Thursday	Friday	Saturday	Notes
6 a.m.				
7 a.m.				
8 a.m.				
9 a.m.				
10 a.m.				
11 a.m.				
12 p.m.				
1 p.m.				
2 p.m.				
3 p.m.				
4 p.m.				
5 p.m.				
6 p.m.				
7 p.m.				
Weather: High Temp: Low Temp:				
Harvest Yield				

WEEK AT A GLANCE FOR _____

	Sunday	Monday	Tuesday	Wednesday
6 a.m.				
7 a.m.				
8 a.m.				
9 a.m.				
10 a.m.				
11 a.m.				
12 p.m.				
1 p.m.				
2 p.m.				
3 p.m.				
4 p.m.				
5 p.m.				
6 p.m.				
7 p.m.				
Weather: High Temp: Low Temp:				
Harvest Yield				

 **WEEK AT A GLANCE FOR** _____

	Thursday	Friday	Saturday	Notes
6 a.m.				
7 a.m.				
8 a.m.				
9 a.m.				
10 a.m.				
11 a.m.				
12 p.m.				
1 p.m.				
2 p.m.				
3 p.m.				
4 p.m.				
5 p.m.				
6 p.m.				
7 p.m.				
Weather: High Temp: Low Temp:				
Harvest Yield				

 **WEEK AT A GLANCE FOR** _____

	Sunday	Monday	Tuesday	Wednesday
6 a.m.				
7 a.m.				
8 a.m.				
9 a.m.				
10 a.m.				
11 a.m.				
12 p.m.				
1 p.m.				
2 p.m.				
3 p.m.				
4 p.m.				
5 p.m.				
6 p.m.				
7 p.m.				
Weather: High Temp: Low Temp:				
Harvest Yield				

 **WEEK AT A GLANCE FOR** _____

	Thursday	Friday	Saturday	Notes
6 a.m.				
7 a.m.				
8 a.m.				
9 a.m.				
10 a.m.				
11 a.m.				
12 p.m.				
1 p.m.				
2 p.m.				
3 p.m.				
4 p.m.				
5 p.m.				
6 p.m.				
7 p.m.				
Weather: High Temp: Low Temp:				
Harvest Yield				

WEEK AT A GLANCE FOR _____

	Sunday	Monday	Tuesday	Wednesday
6 a.m.				
7 a.m.				
8 a.m.				
9 a.m.				
10 a.m.				
11 a.m.				
12 p.m.				
1 p.m.				
2 p.m.				
3 p.m.				
4 p.m.				
5 p.m.				
6 p.m.				
7 p.m.				
Weather: High Temp: Low Temp:				
Harvest Yield				

WEEK AT A GLANCE FOR _____

	Thursday	Friday	Saturday	Notes
6 a.m.				
7 a.m.				
8 a.m.				
9 a.m.				
10 a.m.				
11 a.m.				
12 p.m.				
1 p.m.				
2 p.m.				
3 p.m.				
4 p.m.				
5 p.m.				
6 p.m.				
7 p.m.				
Weather: High Temp: Low Temp:				
Harvest Yield				

MONTH AT A GLANCE FOR _____

Sunday	Monday	Tuesday	Wednesday

Thursday	Friday	Saturday	Notes

MONTHLY PLANNING FOR _____

(See part 3, "Monthly Gardening Tasks by Zone")

Garden Tasks for the Month

Must-Do Projects

Notes

MONTHLY EXPENSES

Date	Paid to	Item	Amt.	Yield (if applicable)

 **WEEK AT A GLANCE FOR** _____

	Sunday	Monday	Tuesday	Wednesday
6 a.m.				
7 a.m.				
8 a.m.				
9 a.m.				
10 a.m.				
11 a.m.				
12 p.m.				
1 p.m.				
2 p.m.				
3 p.m.				
4 p.m.				
5 p.m.				
6 p.m.				
7 p.m.				
Weather: High Temp: Low Temp:				
Menu Plan				

WEEK AT A GLANCE FOR _____

	Thursday	Friday	Saturday	Notes
6 a.m.				
7 a.m.				
8 a.m.				
9 a.m.				
10 a.m.				
11 a.m.				
12 p.m.				
1 p.m.				
2 p.m.				
3 p.m.				
4 p.m.				
5 p.m.				
6 p.m.				
7 p.m.				
Weather: High Temp: Low Temp:				
Harvest Yield				

 # WEEK AT A GLANCE FOR _____

	Sunday	Monday	Tuesday	Wednesday
6 a.m.				
7 a.m.				
8 a.m.				
9 a.m.				
10 a.m.				
11 a.m.				
12 p.m.				
1 p.m.				
2 p.m.				
3 p.m.				
4 p.m.				
5 p.m.				
6 p.m.				
7 p.m.				
Weather: High Temp: Low Temp:				
Harvest Yield				

WEEK AT A GLANCE FOR _____

	Thursday	Friday	Saturday	Notes
6 a.m.				
7 a.m.				
8 a.m.				
9 a.m.				
10 a.m.				
11 a.m.				
12 p.m.				
1 p.m.				
2 p.m.				
3 p.m.				
4 p.m.				
5 p.m.				
6 p.m.				
7 p.m.				
Weather: High Temp: Low Temp:				
Harvest Yield				

 **WEEK AT A GLANCE FOR** _____

	Sunday	Monday	Tuesday	Wednesday
6 a.m.				
7 a.m.				
8 a.m.				
9 a.m.				
10 a.m.				
11 a.m.				
12 p.m.				
1 p.m.				
2 p.m.				
3 p.m.				
4 p.m.				
5 p.m.				
6 p.m.				
7 p.m.				
Weather: High Temp: Low Temp:				
Harvest Yield				

WEEK AT A GLANCE FOR _____

	Thursday	Friday	Saturday	Notes
6 a.m.				
7 a.m.				
8 a.m.				
9 a.m.				
10 a.m.				
11 a.m.				
12 p.m.				
1 p.m.				
2 p.m.				
3 p.m.				
4 p.m.				
5 p.m.				
6 p.m.				
7 p.m.				
Weather: High Temp: Low Temp:				
Harvest Yield				

 **WEEK AT A GLANCE FOR** _____

	Sunday	Monday	Tuesday	Wednesday
6 a.m.				
7 a.m.				
8 a.m.				
9 a.m.				
10 a.m.				
11 a.m.				
12 p.m.				
1 p.m.				
2 p.m.				
3 p.m.				
4 p.m.				
5 p.m.				
6 p.m.				
7 p.m.				
Weather: High Temp: Low Temp:				
Harvest Yield				

 # WEEK AT A GLANCE FOR _____

	Thursday	Friday	Saturday	Notes
6 a.m.				
7 a.m.				
8 a.m.				
9 a.m.				
10 a.m.				
11 a.m.				
12 p.m.				
1 p.m.				
2 p.m.				
3 p.m.				
4 p.m.				
5 p.m.				
6 p.m.				
7 p.m.				
Weather: High Temp: Low Temp:				
Harvest Yield				

WEEK AT A GLANCE FOR _____

	Sunday	Monday	Tuesday	Wednesday
6 a.m.				
7 a.m.				
8 a.m.				
9 a.m.				
10 a.m.				
11 a.m.				
12 p.m.				
1 p.m.				
2 p.m.				
3 p.m.				
4 p.m.				
5 p.m.				
6 p.m.				
7 p.m.				
Weather: High Temp: Low Temp:				
Harvest Yield				

WEEK AT A GLANCE FOR _____

	Thursday	Friday	Saturday	Notes
6 a.m.				
7 a.m.				
8 a.m.				
9 a.m.				
10 a.m.				
11 a.m.				
12 p.m.				
1 p.m.				
2 p.m.				
3 p.m.				
4 p.m.				
5 p.m.				
6 p.m.				
7 p.m.				
Weather: High Temp: Low Temp:				
Harvest Yield				

MONTH AT A GLANCE FOR _____

Sunday	Monday	Tuesday	Wednesday

Thursday	Friday	Saturday	Notes

MONTHLY PLANNING FOR _____

(See part 3, "Monthly Gardening Tasks by Zone")

Garden Tasks for the Month

Must-Do Projects

Notes

MONTHLY EXPENSES

Date	Paid to	Item	Amt.	Yield (if applicable)

WEEK AT A GLANCE FOR _____

	Sunday	Monday	Tuesday	Wednesday
6 a.m.				
7 a.m.				
8 a.m.				
9 a.m.				
10 a.m.				
11 a.m.				
12 p.m.				
1 p.m.				
2 p.m.				
3 p.m.				
4 p.m.				
5 p.m.				
6 p.m.				
7 p.m.				
Weather: High Temp: Low Temp:				
Harvest Yield				

WEEK AT A GLANCE FOR _____

	Thursday	Friday	Saturday	Notes
6 a.m.				
7 a.m.				
8 a.m.				
9 a.m.				
10 a.m.				
11 a.m.				
12 p.m.				
1 p.m.				
2 p.m.				
3 p.m.				
4 p.m.				
5 p.m.				
6 p.m.				
7 p.m.				
Weather: High Temp: Low Temp:				
Harvest Yield				

 **WEEK AT A GLANCE FOR** _____

	Sunday	Monday	Tuesday	Wednesday
6 a.m.				
7 a.m.				
8 a.m.				
9 a.m.				
10 a.m.				
11 a.m.				
12 p.m.				
1 p.m.				
2 p.m.				
3 p.m.				
4 p.m.				
5 p.m.				
6 p.m.				
7 p.m.				
Weather: High Temp: Low Temp:				
Harvest Yield				

 **WEEK AT A GLANCE FOR** _____

	Thursday	Friday	Saturday	Notes
6 a.m.				
7 a.m.				
8 a.m.				
9 a.m.				
10 a.m.				
11 a.m.				
12 p.m.				
1 p.m.				
2 p.m.				
3 p.m.				
4 p.m.				
5 p.m.				
6 p.m.				
7 p.m.				
Weather: High Temp: Low Temp:				
Harvest Yield				

 **WEEK AT A GLANCE FOR** _____

	Sunday	Monday	Tuesday	Wednesday
6 a.m.				
7 a.m.				
8 a.m.				
9 a.m.				
10 a.m.				
11 a.m.				
12 p.m.				
1 p.m.				
2 p.m.				
3 p.m.				
4 p.m.				
5 p.m.				
6 p.m.				
7 p.m.				
Weather: High Temp: Low Temp:				
Harvest Yield				

WEEK AT A GLANCE FOR _____

	Thursday	Friday	Saturday	Notes
6 a.m.				
7 a.m.				
8 a.m.				
9 a.m.				
10 a.m.				
11 a.m.				
12 p.m.				
1 p.m.				
2 p.m.				
3 p.m.				
4 p.m.				
5 p.m.				
6 p.m.				
7 p.m.				
Weather: High Temp: Low Temp:				
Harvest Yield				

 **WEEK AT A GLANCE FOR** _____

	Sunday	Monday	Tuesday	Wednesday
6 a.m.				
7 a.m.				
8 a.m.				
9 a.m.				
10 a.m.				
11 a.m.				
12 p.m.				
1 p.m.				
2 p.m.				
3 p.m.				
4 p.m.				
5 p.m.				
6 p.m.				
7 p.m.				
Weather: High Temp: Low Temp:				
Harvest Yield				

WEEK AT A GLANCE FOR _____

	Thursday	Friday	Saturday	Notes
6 a.m.				
7 a.m.				
8 a.m.				
9 a.m.				
10 a.m.				
11 a.m.				
12 p.m.				
1 p.m.				
2 p.m.				
3 p.m.				
4 p.m.				
5 p.m.				
6 p.m.				
7 p.m.				
Weather: High Temp: Low Temp:				
Harvest Yield				

 # WEEK AT A GLANCE FOR _____

	Sunday	Monday	Tuesday	Wednesday
6 a.m.				
7 a.m.				
8 a.m.				
9 a.m.				
10 a.m.				
11 a.m.				
12 p.m.				
1 p.m.				
2 p.m.				
3 p.m.				
4 p.m.				
5 p.m.				
6 p.m.				
7 p.m.				
Weather: High Temp: Low Temp:				
Harvest Yield				

 **WEEK AT A GLANCE FOR** _____

	Thursday	Friday	Saturday	Notes
6 a.m.				
7 a.m.				
8 a.m.				
9 a.m.				
10 a.m.				
11 a.m.				
12 p.m.				
1 p.m.				
2 p.m.				
3 p.m.				
4 p.m.				
5 p.m.				
6 p.m.				
7 p.m.				
Weather: High Temp: Low Temp:				
Harvest Yield				

MONTH AT A GLANCE FOR _____

Sunday	Monday	Tuesday	Wednesday

Thursday	Friday	Saturday	Notes

MONTHLY PLANNING FOR _____

(See part 3, "Monthly Gardening Tasks by Zone")

Garden Tasks for the Month

Must-Do Projects

Notes

MONTHLY EXPENSES

Date	Paid to	Item	Amt.	Yield (if applicable)

WEEK AT A GLANCE FOR _____

	Sunday	Monday	Tuesday	Wednesday
6 a.m.				
7 a.m.				
8 a.m.				
9 a.m.				
10 a.m.				
11 a.m.				
12 p.m.				
1 p.m.				
2 p.m.				
3 p.m.				
4 p.m.				
5 p.m.				
6 p.m.				
7 p.m.				
Weather: High Temp: Low Temp:				
Harvest Yield				

WEEK AT A GLANCE FOR _____

	Thursday	Friday	Saturday	Notes
6 a.m.				
7 a.m.				
8 a.m.				
9 a.m.				
10 a.m.				
11 a.m.				
12 p.m.				
1 p.m.				
2 p.m.				
3 p.m.				
4 p.m.				
5 p.m.				
6 p.m.				
7 p.m.				
Weather: High Temp: Low Temp:				
Harvest Yield				

 # WEEK AT A GLANCE FOR _____

	Sunday	Monday	Tuesday	Wednesday
6 a.m.				
7 a.m.				
8 a.m.				
9 a.m.				
10 a.m.				
11 a.m.				
12 p.m.				
1 p.m.				
2 p.m.				
3 p.m.				
4 p.m.				
5 p.m.				
6 p.m.				
7 p.m.				
Weather: High Temp: Low Temp:				
Harvest Yield				

 **WEEK AT A GLANCE FOR** _____

	Thursday	Friday	Saturday	Notes
6 a.m.				
7 a.m.				
8 a.m.				
9 a.m.				
10 a.m.				
11 a.m.				
12 p.m.				
1 p.m.				
2 p.m.				
3 p.m.				
4 p.m.				
5 p.m.				
6 p.m.				
7 p.m.				
Weather: High Temp: Low Temp:				
Harvest Yield				

WEEK AT A GLANCE FOR _____

	Sunday	Monday	Tuesday	Wednesday
6 a.m.				
7 a.m.				
8 a.m.				
9 a.m.				
10 a.m.				
11 a.m.				
12 p.m.				
1 p.m.				
2 p.m.				
3 p.m.				
4 p.m.				
5 p.m.				
6 p.m.				
7 p.m.				
Weather: High Temp: Low Temp:				
Harvest Yield				

WEEK AT A GLANCE FOR _____

	Thursday	Friday	Saturday	Notes
6 a.m.				
7 a.m.				
8 a.m.				
9 a.m.				
10 a.m.				
11 a.m.				
12 p.m.				
1 p.m.				
2 p.m.				
3 p.m.				
4 p.m.				
5 p.m.				
6 p.m.				
7 p.m.				
Weather: High Temp: Low Temp:				
Harvest Yield				

WEEK AT A GLANCE FOR _____

	Sunday	Monday	Tuesday	Wednesday
6 a.m.				
7 a.m.				
8 a.m.				
9 a.m.				
10 a.m.				
11 a.m.				
12 p.m.				
1 p.m.				
2 p.m.				
3 p.m.				
4 p.m.				
5 p.m.				
6 p.m.				
7 p.m.				
Weather: High Temp: Low Temp:				
Harvest Yield				

WEEK AT A GLANCE FOR _____

	Thursday	Friday	Saturday	Notes
6 a.m.				
7 a.m.				
8 a.m.				
9 a.m.				
10 a.m.				
11 a.m.				
12 p.m.				
1 p.m.				
2 p.m.				
3 p.m.				
4 p.m.				
5 p.m.				
6 p.m.				
7 p.m.				
Weather: High Temp: Low Temp:				
Harvest Yield				

WEEK AT A GLANCE FOR _____

	Sunday	Monday	Tuesday	Wednesday
6 a.m.				
7 a.m.				
8 a.m.				
9 a.m.				
10 a.m.				
11 a.m.				
12 p.m.				
1 p.m.				
2 p.m.				
3 p.m.				
4 p.m.				
5 p.m.				
6 p.m.				
7 p.m.				
Weather: High Temp: Low Temp:				
Harvest Yield				

WEEK AT A GLANCE FOR _____

	Thursday	Friday	Saturday	Notes
6 a.m.				
7 a.m.				
8 a.m.				
9 a.m.				
10 a.m.				
11 a.m.				
12 p.m.				
1 p.m.				
2 p.m.				
3 p.m.				
4 p.m.				
5 p.m.				
6 p.m.				
7 p.m.				
Weather: High Temp: Low Temp:				
Harvest Yield				

MONTH AT A GLANCE FOR _____

Sunday	Monday	Tuesday	Wednesday

Thursday	Friday	Saturday	Notes

MONTHLY PLANNING FOR _____

(See part 3, "Monthly Gardening Tasks by Zone")

Garden Tasks for the Month

Must-Do Projects

Notes

MONTHLY EXPENSES

Date	Paid to	Item	Amt.	Yield (if applicable)

WEEK AT A GLANCE FOR _____

	Sunday	Monday	Tuesday	Wednesday
6 a.m.				
7 a.m.				
8 a.m.				
9 a.m.				
10 a.m.				
11 a.m.				
12 p.m.				
1 p.m.				
2 p.m.				
3 p.m.				
4 p.m.				
5 p.m.				
6 p.m.				
7 p.m.				
Weather: High Temp: Low Temp:				
Harvest Yield				

WEEK AT A GLANCE FOR _____

	Thursday	Friday	Saturday	Notes
6 a.m.				
7 a.m.				
8 a.m.				
9 a.m.				
10 a.m.				
11 a.m.				
12 p.m.				
1 p.m.				
2 p.m.				
3 p.m.				
4 p.m.				
5 p.m.				
6 p.m.				
7 p.m.				
Weather: High Temp: Low Temp:				
Harvest Yield				

 # WEEK AT A GLANCE FOR _____

	Sunday	Monday	Tuesday	Wednesday
6 a.m.				
7 a.m.				
8 a.m.				
9 a.m.				
10 a.m.				
11 a.m.				
12 p.m.				
1 p.m.				
2 p.m.				
3 p.m.				
4 p.m.				
5 p.m.				
6 p.m.				
7 p.m.				
Weather: High Temp: Low Temp:				
Harvest Yield				

 **WEEK AT A GLANCE FOR** _____

	Thursday	Friday	Saturday	Notes
6 a.m.				
7 a.m.				
8 a.m.				
9 a.m.				
10 a.m.				
11 a.m.				
12 p.m.				
1 p.m.				
2 p.m.				
3 p.m.				
4 p.m.				
5 p.m.				
6 p.m.				
7 p.m.				
Weather: High Temp: Low Temp:				
Harvest Yield				

WEEK AT A GLANCE FOR _____

	Sunday	Monday	Tuesday	Wednesday
6 a.m.				
7 a.m.				
8 a.m.				
9 a.m.				
10 a.m.				
11 a.m.				
12 p.m.				
1 p.m.				
2 p.m.				
3 p.m.				
4 p.m.				
5 p.m.				
6 p.m.				
7 p.m.				
Weather: High Temp: Low Temp:				
Harvest Yield				

WEEK AT A GLANCE FOR _____

	Thursday	Friday	Saturday	Notes
6 a.m.				
7 a.m.				
8 a.m.				
9 a.m.				
10 a.m.				
11 a.m.				
12 p.m.				
1 p.m.				
2 p.m.				
3 p.m.				
4 p.m.				
5 p.m.				
6 p.m.				
7 p.m.				
Weather: High Temp: Low Temp:				
Harvest Yield				

 **WEEK AT A GLANCE FOR** _____

	Sunday	Monday	Tuesday	Wednesday
6 a.m.				
7 a.m.				
8 a.m.				
9 a.m.				
10 a.m.				
11 a.m.				
12 p.m.				
1 p.m.				
2 p.m.				
3 p.m.				
4 p.m.				
5 p.m.				
6 p.m.				
7 p.m.				
Weather: High Temp: Low Temp:				
Harvest Yield				

WEEK AT A GLANCE FOR _____

	Thursday	Friday	Saturday	Notes
6 a.m.				
7 a.m.				
8 a.m.				
9 a.m.				
10 a.m.				
11 a.m.				
12 p.m.				
1 p.m.				
2 p.m.				
3 p.m.				
4 p.m.				
5 p.m.				
6 p.m.				
7 p.m.				
Weather: High Temp: Low Temp:				
Harvest Yield				

 **WEEK AT A GLANCE FOR** _____

	Sunday	Monday	Tuesday	Wednesday
6 a.m.				
7 a.m.				
8 a.m.				
9 a.m.				
10 a.m.				
11 a.m.				
12 p.m.				
1 p.m.				
2 p.m.				
3 p.m.				
4 p.m.				
5 p.m.				
6 p.m.				
7 p.m.				
Weather: High Temp: Low Temp:				
Harvest Yield				

WEEK AT A GLANCE FOR _____

	Thursday	Friday	Saturday	Notes
6 a.m.				
7 a.m.				
8 a.m.				
9 a.m.				
10 a.m.				
11 a.m.				
12 p.m.				
1 p.m.				
2 p.m.				
3 p.m.				
4 p.m.				
5 p.m.				
6 p.m.				
7 p.m.				
Weather: High Temp: Low Temp:				
Harvest Yield				

MONTH AT A GLANCE FOR _____

Sunday	Monday	Tuesday	Wednesday

Thursday	Friday	Saturday	Notes

MONTHLY PLANNING FOR _____

(See part 3, "Monthly Gardening Tasks by Zone")

Garden Tasks for the Month

Must-Do Projects

Notes

MONTHLY EXPENSES

Date	Paid to	Item	Amt.	Yield (if applicable)

 **WEEK AT A GLANCE FOR** _____

	Sunday	Monday	Tuesday	Wednesday
6 a.m.				
7 a.m.				
8 a.m.				
9 a.m.				
10 a.m.				
11 a.m.				
12 p.m.				
1 p.m.				
2 p.m.				
3 p.m.				
4 p.m.				
5 p.m.				
6 p.m.				
7 p.m.				
Weather: High Temp: Low Temp:				
Harvest Yield				

 **WEEK AT A GLANCE FOR** _____

	Thursday	Friday	Saturday	Notes
6 a.m.				
7 a.m.				
8 a.m.				
9 a.m.				
10 a.m.				
11 a.m.				
12 p.m.				
1 p.m.				
2 p.m.				
3 p.m.				
4 p.m.				
5 p.m.				
6 p.m.				
7 p.m.				
Weather: High Temp: Low Temp:				
Harvest Yield				

 **WEEK AT A GLANCE FOR** _____

	Sunday	Monday	Tuesday	Wednesday
6 a.m.				
7 a.m.				
8 a.m.				
9 a.m.				
10 a.m.				
11 a.m.				
12 p.m.				
1 p.m.				
2 p.m.				
3 p.m.				
4 p.m.				
5 p.m.				
6 p.m.				
7 p.m.				
Weather: High Temp: Low Temp:				
Harvest Yield				

WEEK AT A GLANCE FOR _____

	Thursday	Friday	Saturday	Notes
6 a.m.				
7 a.m.				
8 a.m.				
9 a.m.				
10 a.m.				
11 a.m.				
12 p.m.				
1 p.m.				
2 p.m.				
3 p.m.				
4 p.m.				
5 p.m.				
6 p.m.				
7 p.m.				
Weather: High Temp: Low Temp:				
Harvest Yield				

 WEEK AT A GLANCE FOR _____

	Sunday	Monday	Tuesday	Wednesday
6 a.m.				
7 a.m.				
8 a.m.				
9 a.m.				
10 a.m.				
11 a.m.				
12 p.m.				
1 p.m.				
2 p.m.				
3 p.m.				
4 p.m.				
5 p.m.				
6 p.m.				
7 p.m.				
Weather: High Temp: Low Temp:				
Harvest Yield				

 **WEEK AT A GLANCE FOR** _____

	Thursday	Friday	Saturday	Notes
6 a.m.				
7 a.m.				
8 a.m.				
9 a.m.				
10 a.m.				
11 a.m.				
12 p.m.				
1 p.m.				
2 p.m.				
3 p.m.				
4 p.m.				
5 p.m.				
6 p.m.				
7 p.m.				
Weather: High Temp: Low Temp:				
Harvest Yield				

WEEK AT A GLANCE FOR _____

	Sunday	Monday	Tuesday	Wednesday
6 a.m.				
7 a.m.				
8 a.m.				
9 a.m.				
10 a.m.				
11 a.m.				
12 p.m.				
1 p.m.				
2 p.m.				
3 p.m.				
4 p.m.				
5 p.m.				
6 p.m.				
7 p.m.				
Weather: High Temp: Low Temp:				
Harvest Yield				

 **WEEK AT A GLANCE FOR** _____

	Thursday	Friday	Saturday	Notes
6 a.m.				
7 a.m.				
8 a.m.				
9 a.m.				
10 a.m.				
11 a.m.				
12 p.m.				
1 p.m.				
2 p.m.				
3 p.m.				
4 p.m.				
5 p.m.				
6 p.m.				
7 p.m.				
Weather: High Temp: Low Temp:				
Harvest Yield				

 **WEEK AT A GLANCE FOR** _____

	Sunday	Monday	Tuesday	Wednesday
6 a.m.				
7 a.m.				
8 a.m.				
9 a.m.				
10 a.m.				
11 a.m.				
12 p.m.				
1 p.m.				
2 p.m.				
3 p.m.				
4 p.m.				
5 p.m.				
6 p.m.				
7 p.m.				
Weather: High Temp: Low Temp:				
Harvest Yield				

WEEK AT A GLANCE FOR _____

	Thursday	Friday	Saturday	Notes
6 a.m.				
7 a.m.				
8 a.m.				
9 a.m.				
10 a.m.				
11 a.m.				
12 p.m.				
1 p.m.				
2 p.m.				
3 p.m.				
4 p.m.				
5 p.m.				
6 p.m.				
7 p.m.				
Weather: High Temp: Low Temp:				
Harvest Yield				

MONTH AT A GLANCE FOR _____

Sunday	Monday	Tuesday	Wednesday

Thursday	Friday	Saturday	Notes

MONTHLY PLANNING FOR _____

(See part 3, "Monthly Gardening Tasks by Zone")

Garden Tasks for the Month

Must-Do Projects

Notes

MONTHLY EXPENSES

Date	Paid to	Item	Amt.	Yield (if applicable)

 **WEEK AT A GLANCE FOR** _____

	Sunday	Monday	Tuesday	Wednesday
6 a.m.				
7 a.m.				
8 a.m.				
9 a.m.				
10 a.m.				
11 a.m.				
12 p.m.				
1 p.m.				
2 p.m.				
3 p.m.				
4 p.m.				
5 p.m.				
6 p.m.				
7 p.m.				
Weather: High Temp: Low Temp:				
Harvest Yield				

WEEK AT A GLANCE FOR _____

	Thursday	Friday	Saturday	Notes
6 a.m.				
7 a.m.				
8 a.m.				
9 a.m.				
10 a.m.				
11 a.m.				
12 p.m.				
1 p.m.				
2 p.m.				
3 p.m.				
4 p.m.				
5 p.m.				
6 p.m.				
7 p.m.				
Weather: High Temp: Low Temp:				
Harvest Yield				

WEEK AT A GLANCE FOR _____

	Sunday	Monday	Tuesday	Wednesday
6 a.m.				
7 a.m.				
8 a.m.				
9 a.m.				
10 a.m.				
11 a.m.				
12 p.m.				
1 p.m.				
2 p.m.				
3 p.m.				
4 p.m.				
5 p.m.				
6 p.m.				
7 p.m.				
Weather: High Temp: Low Temp:				
Harvest Yield				

WEEK AT A GLANCE FOR _____

	Thursday	Friday	Saturday	Notes
6 a.m.				
7 a.m.				
8 a.m.				
9 a.m.				
10 a.m.				
11 a.m.				
12 p.m.				
1 p.m.				
2 p.m.				
3 p.m.				
4 p.m.				
5 p.m.				
6 p.m.				
7 p.m.				
Weather: High Temp: Low Temp:				
Harvest Yield				

WEEK AT A GLANCE FOR _____

	Sunday	Monday	Tuesday	Wednesday
6 a.m.				
7 a.m.				
8 a.m.				
9 a.m.				
10 a.m.				
11 a.m.				
12 p.m.				
1 p.m.				
2 p.m.				
3 p.m.				
4 p.m.				
5 p.m.				
6 p.m.				
7 p.m.				
Weather: High Temp: Low Temp:				
Harvest Yield				

 **WEEK AT A GLANCE FOR** _____

	Thursday	Friday	Saturday	Notes
6 a.m.				
7 a.m.				
8 a.m.				
9 a.m.				
10 a.m.				
11 a.m.				
12 p.m.				
1 p.m.				
2 p.m.				
3 p.m.				
4 p.m.				
5 p.m.				
6 p.m.				
7 p.m.				
Weather: High Temp: Low Temp:				
Harvest Yield				

 **WEEK AT A GLANCE FOR** _____

	Sunday	Monday	Tuesday	Wednesday
6 a.m.				
7 a.m.				
8 a.m.				
9 a.m.				
10 a.m.				
11 a.m.				
12 p.m.				
1 p.m.				
2 p.m.				
3 p.m.				
4 p.m.				
5 p.m.				
6 p.m.				
7 p.m.				
Weather: High Temp: Low Temp:				
Harvest Yield				

WEEK AT A GLANCE FOR _____

	Thursday	Friday	Saturday	Notes
6 a.m.				
7 a.m.				
8 a.m.				
9 a.m.				
10 a.m.				
11 a.m.				
12 p.m.				
1 p.m.				
2 p.m.				
3 p.m.				
4 p.m.				
5 p.m.				
6 p.m.				
7 p.m.				
Weather: High Temp: Low Temp:				
Harvest Yield				

 **WEEK AT A GLANCE FOR** _____

	Sunday	Monday	Tuesday	Wednesday
6 a.m.				
7 a.m.				
8 a.m.				
9 a.m.				
10 a.m.				
11 a.m.				
12 p.m.				
1 p.m.				
2 p.m.				
3 p.m.				
4 p.m.				
5 p.m.				
6 p.m.				
7 p.m.				
Weather: High Temp: Low Temp:				
Harvest Yield				

WEEK AT A GLANCE FOR _____

	Thursday	Friday	Saturday	Notes
6 a.m.				
7 a.m.				
8 a.m.				
9 a.m.				
10 a.m.				
11 a.m.				
12 p.m.				
1 p.m.				
2 p.m.				
3 p.m.				
4 p.m.				
5 p.m.				
6 p.m.				
7 p.m.				
Weather: High Temp: Low Temp:				
Harvest Yield				

MONTH AT A GLANCE FOR _____

Sunday	Monday	Tuesday	Wednesday

Thursday	Friday	Saturday	Notes

MONTHLY PLANNING FOR _____

(See part 3, "Monthly Gardening Tasks by Zone")

Garden Tasks for the Month

Must-Do Projects

Notes

MONTHLY EXPENSES

Date	Paid to	Item	Amt.	Yield (if applicable)

 **WEEK AT A GLANCE FOR** _____

	Sunday	Monday	Tuesday	Wednesday
6 a.m.				
7 a.m.				
8 a.m.				
9 a.m.				
10 a.m.				
11 a.m.				
12 p.m.				
1 p.m.				
2 p.m.				
3 p.m.				
4 p.m.				
5 p.m.				
6 p.m.				
7 p.m.				
Weather: High Temp: Low Temp:				
Harvest Yield				

 **WEEK AT A GLANCE FOR** _____

	Thursday	Friday	Saturday	Notes
6 a.m.				
7 a.m.				
8 a.m.				
9 a.m.				
10 a.m.				
11 a.m.				
12 p.m.				
1 p.m.				
2 p.m.				
3 p.m.				
4 p.m.				
5 p.m.				
6 p.m.				
7 p.m.				
Weather: High Temp: Low Temp:				
Harvest Yield				

 **WEEK AT A GLANCE FOR** _____

	Sunday	Monday	Tuesday	Wednesday
6 a.m.				
7 a.m.				
8 a.m.				
9 a.m.				
10 a.m.				
11 a.m.				
12 p.m.				
1 p.m.				
2 p.m.				
3 p.m.				
4 p.m.				
5 p.m.				
6 p.m.				
7 p.m.				
Weather: High Temp: Low Temp:				
Harvest Yield				

WEEK AT A GLANCE FOR _____

	Thursday	Friday	Saturday	Notes
6 a.m.				
7 a.m.				
8 a.m.				
9 a.m.				
10 a.m.				
11 a.m.				
12 p.m.				
1 p.m.				
2 p.m.				
3 p.m.				
4 p.m.				
5 p.m.				
6 p.m.				
7 p.m.				
Weather: High Temp: Low Temp:				
Harvest Yield				

 WEEK AT A GLANCE FOR _____

	Sunday	Monday	Tuesday	Wednesday
6 a.m.				
7 a.m.				
8 a.m.				
9 a.m.				
10 a.m.				
11 a.m.				
12 p.m.				
1 p.m.				
2 p.m.				
3 p.m.				
4 p.m.				
5 p.m.				
6 p.m.				
7 p.m.				
Weather: High Temp: Low Temp:				
Harvest Yield				

WEEK AT A GLANCE FOR _____

	Thursday	Friday	Saturday	Notes
6 a.m.				
7 a.m.				
8 a.m.				
9 a.m.				
10 a.m.				
11 a.m.				
12 p.m.				
1 p.m.				
2 p.m.				
3 p.m.				
4 p.m.				
5 p.m.				
6 p.m.				
7 p.m.				
Weather: High Temp: Low Temp:				
Harvest Yield				

WEEK AT A GLANCE FOR _____

	Sunday	Monday	Tuesday	Wednesday
6 a.m.				
7 a.m.				
8 a.m.				
9 a.m.				
10 a.m.				
11 a.m.				
12 p.m.				
1 p.m.				
2 p.m.				
3 p.m.				
4 p.m.				
5 p.m.				
6 p.m.				
7 p.m.				
Weather: High Temp: Low Temp:				
Harvest Yield				

WEEK AT A GLANCE FOR _____

	Thursday	Friday	Saturday	Notes
6 a.m.				
7 a.m.				
8 a.m.				
9 a.m.				
10 a.m.				
11 a.m.				
12 p.m.				
1 p.m.				
2 p.m.				
3 p.m.				
4 p.m.				
5 p.m.				
6 p.m.				
7 p.m.				
Weather: High Temp: Low Temp:				
Harvest Yield				

WEEK AT A GLANCE FOR _____

	Sunday	Monday	Tuesday	Wednesday
6 a.m.				
7 a.m.				
8 a.m.				
9 a.m.				
10 a.m.				
11 a.m.				
12 p.m.				
1 p.m.				
2 p.m.				
3 p.m.				
4 p.m.				
5 p.m.				
6 p.m.				
7 p.m.				
Weather: High Temp: Low Temp:				
Harvest Yield				

WEEK AT A GLANCE FOR _____

	Thursday	Friday	Saturday	Notes
6 a.m.				
7 a.m.				
8 a.m.				
9 a.m.				
10 a.m.				
11 a.m.				
12 p.m.				
1 p.m.				
2 p.m.				
3 p.m.				
4 p.m.				
5 p.m.				
6 p.m.				
7 p.m.				
Weather: High Temp: Low Temp:				
Harvest Yield				

MONTH AT A GLANCE FOR _____

Sunday	Monday	Tuesday	Wednesday

Thursday	Friday	Saturday	Notes

MONTHLY PLANNING FOR _____

(See part 3, "Monthly Gardening Tasks by Zone")

Garden Tasks for the Month

Must-Do Projects

Notes

MONTHLY EXPENSES

Date	Paid to	Item	Amt.	Yield (if applicable)

WEEK AT A GLANCE FOR _____

	Sunday	Monday	Tuesday	Wednesday
6 a.m.				
7 a.m.				
8 a.m.				
9 a.m.				
10 a.m.				
11 a.m.				
12 p.m.				
1 p.m.				
2 p.m.				
3 p.m.				
4 p.m.				
5 p.m.				
6 p.m.				
7 p.m.				
Weather: High Temp: Low Temp:				
Harvest Yield				

 **WEEK AT A GLANCE FOR** _____

	Thursday	Friday	Saturday	Notes
6 a.m.				
7 a.m.				
8 a.m.				
9 a.m.				
10 a.m.				
11 a.m.				
12 p.m.				
1 p.m.				
2 p.m.				
3 p.m.				
4 p.m.				
5 p.m.				
6 p.m.				
7 p.m.				
Weather: High Temp: Low Temp:				
Harvest Yield				

WEEK AT A GLANCE FOR _____

	Sunday	Monday	Tuesday	Wednesday
6 a.m.				
7 a.m.				
8 a.m.				
9 a.m.				
10 a.m.				
11 a.m.				
12 p.m.				
1 p.m.				
2 p.m.				
3 p.m.				
4 p.m.				
5 p.m.				
6 p.m.				
7 p.m.				
Weather: High Temp: Low Temp:				
Harvest Yield				

 **WEEK AT A GLANCE FOR** _____

	Thursday	Friday	Saturday	Notes
6 a.m.				
7 a.m.				
8 a.m.				
9 a.m.				
10 a.m.				
11 a.m.				
12 p.m.				
1 p.m.				
2 p.m.				
3 p.m.				
4 p.m.				
5 p.m.				
6 p.m.				
7 p.m.				
Weather: High Temp: Low Temp:				
Harvest Yield				

 **WEEK AT A GLANCE FOR** _____

	Sunday	Monday	Tuesday	Wednesday
6 a.m.				
7 a.m.				
8 a.m.				
9 a.m.				
10 a.m.				
11 a.m.				
12 p.m.				
1 p.m.				
2 p.m.				
3 p.m.				
4 p.m.				
5 p.m.				
6 p.m.				
7 p.m.				
Weather: High Temp: Low Temp:				
Harvest Yield				

WEEK AT A GLANCE FOR _____

	Thursday	Friday	Saturday	Notes
6 a.m.				
7 a.m.				
8 a.m.				
9 a.m.				
10 a.m.				
11 a.m.				
12 p.m.				
1 p.m.				
2 p.m.				
3 p.m.				
4 p.m.				
5 p.m.				
6 p.m.				
7 p.m.				
Weather: High Temp: Low Temp:				
Harvest Yield				

 **WEEK AT A GLANCE FOR** _____

	Sunday	Monday	Tuesday	Wednesday
6 a.m.				
7 a.m.				
8 a.m.				
9 a.m.				
10 a.m.				
11 a.m.				
12 p.m.				
1 p.m.				
2 p.m.				
3 p.m.				
4 p.m.				
5 p.m.				
6 p.m.				
7 p.m.				
Weather: High Temp: Low Temp:				
Harvest Yield				

WEEK AT A GLANCE FOR _____

	Thursday	Friday	Saturday	Notes
6 a.m.				
7 a.m.				
8 a.m.				
9 a.m.				
10 a.m.				
11 a.m.				
12 p.m.				
1 p.m.				
2 p.m.				
3 p.m.				
4 p.m.				
5 p.m.				
6 p.m.				
7 p.m.				
Weather: High Temp: Low Temp:				
Harvest Yield				

WEEK AT A GLANCE FOR _____

	Sunday	Monday	Tuesday	Wednesday
6 a.m.				
7 a.m.				
8 a.m.				
9 a.m.				
10 a.m.				
11 a.m.				
12 p.m.				
1 p.m.				
2 p.m.				
3 p.m.				
4 p.m.				
5 p.m.				
6 p.m.				
7 p.m.				
Weather: High Temp: Low Temp:				
Harvest Yield				

 WEEK AT A GLANCE FOR _____

	Thursday	Friday	Saturday	Notes
6 a.m.				
7 a.m.				
8 a.m.				
9 a.m.				
10 a.m.				
11 a.m.				
12 p.m.				
1 p.m.				
2 p.m.				
3 p.m.				
4 p.m.				
5 p.m.				
6 p.m.				
7 p.m.				
Weather: High Temp: Low Temp:				
Harvest Yield				

MONTH AT A GLANCE FOR _____

Sunday	Monday	Tuesday	Wednesday

Thursday	Friday	Saturday	Notes

MONTHLY PLANNING FOR _____

(See part 3, "Monthly Gardening Tasks by Zone")

Garden Tasks for the Month

Must-Do Projects

Notes

MONTHLY EXPENSES

Date	Paid to	Item	Amt.	Yield (if applicable)

 **WEEK AT A GLANCE FOR** _____

	Sunday	Monday	Tuesday	Wednesday
6 a.m.				
7 a.m.				
8 a.m.				
9 a.m.				
10 a.m.				
11 a.m.				
12 p.m.				
1 p.m.				
2 p.m.				
3 p.m.				
4 p.m.				
5 p.m.				
6 p.m.				
7 p.m.				
Weather: High Temp: Low Temp:				
Harvest Yield				

 **WEEK AT A GLANCE FOR** _____

	Thursday	Friday	Saturday	Notes
6 a.m.				
7 a.m.				
8 a.m.				
9 a.m.				
10 a.m.				
11 a.m.				
12 p.m.				
1 p.m.				
2 p.m.				
3 p.m.				
4 p.m.				
5 p.m.				
6 p.m.				
7 p.m.				
Weather: High Temp: Low Temp:				
Harvest Yield				

WEEK AT A GLANCE FOR _____

	Sunday	Monday	Tuesday	Wednesday
6 a.m.				
7 a.m.				
8 a.m.				
9 a.m.				
10 a.m.				
11 a.m.				
12 p.m.				
1 p.m.				
2 p.m.				
3 p.m.				
4 p.m.				
5 p.m.				
6 p.m.				
7 p.m.				
Weather: High Temp: Low Temp:				
Harvest Yield				

 **WEEK AT A GLANCE FOR** _____

	Thursday	Friday	Saturday	Notes
6 a.m.				
7 a.m.				
8 a.m.				
9 a.m.				
10 a.m.				
11 a.m.				
12 p.m.				
1 p.m.				
2 p.m.				
3 p.m.				
4 p.m.				
5 p.m.				
6 p.m.				
7 p.m.				
Weather: High Temp: Low Temp:				
Harvest Yield				

 **WEEK AT A GLANCE FOR** _____

	Sunday	Monday	Tuesday	Wednesday
6 a.m.				
7 a.m.				
8 a.m.				
9 a.m.				
10 a.m.				
11 a.m.				
12 p.m.				
1 p.m.				
2 p.m.				
3 p.m.				
4 p.m.				
5 p.m.				
6 p.m.				
7 p.m.				
Weather: High Temp: Low Temp:				
Harvest Yield				

 **WEEK AT A GLANCE FOR** _____

	Thursday	Friday	Saturday	Notes
6 a.m.				
7 a.m.				
8 a.m.				
9 a.m.				
10 a.m.				
11 a.m.				
12 p.m.				
1 p.m.				
2 p.m.				
3 p.m.				
4 p.m.				
5 p.m.				
6 p.m.				
7 p.m.				
Weather: High Temp: Low Temp:				
Harvest Yield				

WEEK AT A GLANCE FOR _____

	Sunday	Monday	Tuesday	Wednesday
6 a.m.				
7 a.m.				
8 a.m.				
9 a.m.				
10 a.m.				
11 a.m.				
12 p.m.				
1 p.m.				
2 p.m.				
3 p.m.				
4 p.m.				
5 p.m.				
6 p.m.				
7 p.m.				
Weather: High Temp: Low Temp:				
Harvest Yield				

WEEK AT A GLANCE FOR _____

	Thursday	Friday	Saturday	Notes
6 a.m.				
7 a.m.				
8 a.m.				
9 a.m.				
10 a.m.				
11 a.m.				
12 p.m.				
1 p.m.				
2 p.m.				
3 p.m.				
4 p.m.				
5 p.m.				
6 p.m.				
7 p.m.				
Weather: High Temp: Low Temp:				
Harvest Yield				

 **WEEK AT A GLANCE FOR** _____

	Sunday	Monday	Tuesday	Wednesday
6 a.m.				
7 a.m.				
8 a.m.				
9 a.m.				
10 a.m.				
11 a.m.				
12 p.m.				
1 p.m.				
2 p.m.				
3 p.m.				
4 p.m.				
5 p.m.				
6 p.m.				
7 p.m.				
Weather: High Temp: Low Temp:				
Harvest Yield				

 WEEK AT A GLANCE FOR _____

	Thursday	Friday	Saturday	Notes
6 a.m.				
7 a.m.				
8 a.m.				
9 a.m.				
10 a.m.				
11 a.m.				
12 p.m.				
1 p.m.				
2 p.m.				
3 p.m.				
4 p.m.				
5 p.m.				
6 p.m.				
7 p.m.				
Weather: High Temp: Low Temp:				
Harvest Yield				

PART THREE

Monthly Gardening Tasks by Zone

The information below is based on the average first and last frost dates of each gardening zone. Remember that these dates are approximate and vary from year to year. Use the Seed Starting and Planting chart on pages 18-20 to calculate your exact planting times, and consider including a two-week buffer in your long-term planning.

ZONES 3-4

January

Plan out what crops you'll be growing this year (use the Crops for a Year Worksheet on page 16). Take inventory of your seeds and order more if necessary.

Plan your garden layout, and use the Seed Starting and Planting Chart on pages 18-20 to schedule your seed starting and transplanting.

Make sure all your tools are clean and sharp.

February

Watch for damage from deer, mice, and voles on fruit trees. Put fencing around trees if needed.

Start onions from seed indoors 10 to 12 weeks before the last frost date.

Start annual flowers and herbs by seed indoors 8 to 12 weeks before the last frost date.

Start cauliflower 8 to 10 weeks before the last frost date.

Prune blueberry plants and apply at least 1 inch of mulch to smother any mummy berry fungus if necessary.

March

Use cold stratification for any flowers or herbs seeds you'll be seed starting indoors, such as feverfew, horehound, hyssop, lavender, marshmallow, and yarrow.

Start eggplant, summer savory, and tomatoes indoors 6 to 8 weeks before the last frost date.

Start peas indoors 8 weeks before the last frost date.

Start broccoli, cabbage, lettuce, okra, and spinach 6 weeks before the last frost date.

Start pepper seeds indoors 4 to 8 weeks before the last frost date.

Plant bare-root fruit trees, berry bushes, and perennials if the ground is workable.

Prune summer-bearing raspberry plants by removing all canes that produced fruit. Leave 3 to 6 strong new canes per linear foot.

Prune everbearing raspberry plants for a summer and fall harvest by removing the portions of primocanes that produced fruit in the fall. Remove all canes that have fully fruited.

Prune everbearing raspberry plants for a fall harvest only to 3 inches above the ground.

Prune blueberry plants and apply at least 1 inch of mulch to smother any mummy berry fungus if necessary.

Lightly prune trailing blackberries to maintain their shape.

Put together a cold frame and place it in your garden where warm-weather crops will be grown.

April

Tap maple trees (high temps must be above freezing and low temps below freezing).

Transplant lettuce and spinach seedlings into the garden under a low tunnel or hoop house.

Start peppers and tomatoes indoors 8 to 10 weeks before the last frost date.

Direct-sow onion bulbs and spinach 6 weeks before the last frost date.

Start basil, cilantro, and kale indoors 4 to 6 weeks before the last frost date.

Start chard indoors 4 weeks before the last frost date.

Start Brussels sprouts, marjoram, and winter and summer squash seeds indoors 2 to 3 weeks before the last frost date.

Transplant cauliflower, lettuce, pea, and spinach seedlings into the garden 4 weeks before the last frost date.

Transplant onion sets into the garden 2 to 4 weeks before the last frost date.

Direct-sow beets, carrots, kale, lettuce, peas, potatoes, radishes, and turnips 2 to 4 weeks before the last frost date.

Plant bare-root fruit trees and berry bushes when the soil is workable (not frozen).

Prune summer-bearing raspberry plants by removing all canes that produced fruit. Leave 3 to 6 strong new canes per linear foot.

Prune everbearing raspberry plants for a summer and fall harvest by removing the portions of primocanes that produced fruit in the fall. Remove all canes that have fully fruited.

Prune everbearing raspberry plants for a fall harvest only to 3 inches above the ground.

Spray fruit trees and bushes before the buds break for specific diseases or pests if necessary.

Direct-sow flower seeds for spring growing, such as arnica, calendula, chamomile, columbine, lupine, and marshmallow.

Prune perennial herbs (such as lavender and rosemary) to retain the shape, size, and health of the plants as needed.

Plant or divide and transplant perennials such as asparagus and rhubarb.

May

Transplant broccoli, cabbage, and kale seedlings to the garden 2 weeks before the last frost date.

Direct-sow cabbage, cauliflower, cilantro, and parsnips 2 weeks before the last frost date.

Start melon seeds indoors on the last frost date.

Transplant beets, chard, and cilantro into the garden on the last frost date.

Start broccoli indoors for a fall garden 14 to 16 weeks before the first frost date.

Begin harvesting young stinging nettle leaves while they are still young and before the flowers head, ideally before they are a foot tall and the top has 2 or 3 sets of leaves. Wear gloves!

Spray fruit trees at blossom time for specific diseases or pests as necessary.

Harvest young red raspberry leaves for tea before the plant begins to flower.

Plant potted fruit trees, berry bushes, and strawberries.

Apply compost around the base of fruit trees.

Harvest dandelion flowers, lamb's-quarter, ramps, stinging nettles, and violets.

Pull weeds.

Turn compost.

Forage wild mushrooms (such as morel).

June

Transplant Brussels sprouts seedlings into the garden 2 weeks after the last frost date.

Transplant basil, marjoram, melon, okra, pepper, squash (summer and winter), and tomato seedlings, and all herbal flowers, into the garden 3 to 4 weeks after the last frost, provided that nights are at least 55 degrees F.

Direct-sow marjoram and summer savory 1 week after the last frost date.

Direct-sow corn 2 weeks after the last frost date.

Direct-sow basil, beans, dill, and sweet potatoes 3 to 4 weeks after the last frost date.

Start cauliflower indoors for a fall garden 12 to 14 weeks before the first frost date.

Transplant broccoli starts into the garden 10 to 12 weeks before the first frost date.

Direct-sow broccoli, chard, parsnips, and peas for a fall harvest 12 weeks before the first frost date.

Direct-sow Brussels sprouts 10 weeks before the first frost date.

Apply netting to fruit bushes and trees as needed to protect from birds, deer, and other pests.

Harvest asparagus, dandelion flowers, lamb's-quarter, ramps, rhubarb, stinging nettles, and violets.

Harvest lavender buds before they bloom for teas and medicinal purposes.

Forage wild mushrooms (such as morel).

Inoculate mushroom logs.

Put out a rain gauge and record the readings in your garden planner.

Pull weeds.

July

Harvest apricots, beans, beets, blackberries, blueberries, broccoli, cabbage, carrots, celery, cherries, cucumbers, nectarines, peas, peppers, potatoes, raspberries, rhubarb, strawberries, summer squash, and tomatoes.

Transplant all warm-weather starts into the garden if you didn't in June.

Transplant cauliflower starts into a fall garden 8 weeks before the first frost date.

Direct-sow carrots 8 to 12 weeks before the first frost date.

Direct-sow beets and radishes 8 weeks before the first frost date.

Direct-sow cabbage, cilantro, kale, lettuce, and spinach 6 to 8 weeks before the first frost date.

Purchase seed garlic if needed.

Pull weeds.

Water well when needed.

Sow fall and winter cover crops if you're using them.

Harvest herbal flower blossoms for tea and salves.

August

Plant garlic in late August if the ground is frozen by September. Direct-sow garlic cloves 2 weeks before the first frost date to 2 weeks after it.

Direct-sow turnips 4 weeks before the first frost date.

Harvest apples, apricots, beans, beets, blackberries, blueberries, broccoli, cabbage, carrots, celery, corn, cucumbers, nectarines, pears, peas, peppers, potatoes, raspberries, rhubarb, strawberries, summer squash, tomatoes, and winter squash.

If the tops of onions have fallen over, harvest and cure them.

If soft-neck garlic tops have fallen over, harvest and cure them. If the top 2 or 3 sets of leaves on hard-neck garlic have turned brown, harvest and cure them.

Pull up walking (or Egyptian) onions, clip the tops, and allow the tops and bottoms to dry until October.

Harvest herbal flower blossoms for tea and salves.

Harvest purslane tips.

Check routinely for insects and other garden pests.

Pull weeds.

Water.

Watch for powdery mildew.

Fertilize containers.

Turn compost.

Cut to the ground any root suckers near trees.

Place netting over fruit trees and bushes as the fruit ripens to prevent bird damage.

September

Plant garlic if you didn't plant it in August.

Harvest apples, beans, beets, broccoli, Brussels sprouts, cabbage, carrots, corn, cucumbers, elderberries, nectarines, pears, peppers, plums, fall raspberries, rhubarb, summer squash, and tomatoes.

Harvest and cure potatoes and winter squash.

Collect seeds from garden plants and herbs.

Cut back comfrey. Use it as mulch or compost, or give it to your chickens as fodder.

Harvest herbs.

Check routinely for insects and other pests in the garden.

Pull weeds.

Water.

Watch for powdery mildew.

Fertilize containers.

Turn compost.

Place netting over fruit trees and bushes as the fruit ripens to prevent bird damage.

Watch for first frost warning and use any crop extenders on warm-weather crops to extend the season if desired.

Apply compost or manure on perennial plants. If you're using sheet compost or mulch, apply it to your garden beds to protect the soil over the winter.

Apply straw or mulch to any plants that need protection from winter temps.

Start a compost pile with fall leaves and grass clippings.

Perform a fall soil test.

Cut back asparagus ferns after the frost kill, apply compost or manure, and mulch if necessary.

Apply mulch to the base of fruit trees and bushes to help protect roots from winter freeze damage. (Don't allow mulch to girdle the tree trunk.)

Harvest echinacea root on 3-year-old or older plants after the first frost date.

Harvest dandelion roots before the ground freezes.

Spray fruit trees and bushes for specific diseases or pests as necessary.

Forage wild mushrooms (such as chanterelle, chicken of the woods, lion's mane, lobster, oyster, and porcini).

Cut off the tips of blackberry primocanes to increase the fruit yield. For everbearing blackberry primocanes that have fruited, prune them back to the ground for a fall harvest only.

Pull weeds before prepping your garden beds for winter. Build up the soil by covering it with fallen leaves, compost, natural fertilizers (such as chicken manure), and so on.

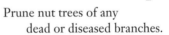

Clean up and remove any fallen fruit. Decaying fruit will harbor disease and pests.

Prune nut trees of any dead or diseased branches.

Drain your garden hoses and sprinklers and store them for winter.

Turn compost.

October

Apply tree wraps to help protect trees from winter damage.

November

NA

December

NA

ZONES 5-6

January

Plan out what crops you'll be growing this year (use the Crops for a Year worksheet on page 16). Take inventory of your seeds and order more if necessary.

Plan your garden layout, and use the Seed Starting and Planting chart on pages 18-20 to schedule your seed starting and transplanting.

Make sure all your tools are clean and sharp.

Watch for damage from deer, mice, and voles on fruit trees and bushes. Erect fencing if necessary.

February

Use cold stratification for any flowers or herbs seeds you'll be seed starting indoors, such as feverfew, horehound, hyssop, lavender, marshmallow, and yarrow.

Put together a cold frame and place it in your garden where warm-weather crops will be grown.

Tap maple trees (high temps must be above freezing and low temps below freezing).

Prune blueberry plants and apply at least 1 inch of mulch to smother any mummy berry fungus if applicable.

Spray fruit trees and bushes before the buds break for specific diseases or pests if necessary.

Direct-sow flower seeds for spring growing, such as arnica, calendula, chamomile, columbine, lupine, and marshmallow.

March

Start celery and onion seeds indoors 10 to 12 weeks before the last frost date.

Start broccoli, Brussels sprouts, cabbage, lettuce, okra, and spinach indoors 6 to 12 weeks before the last frost date.

Start peppers indoors 4 to 8 weeks before the last frost date.

Start eggplant, summer savory, and tomatoes indoors 6 to 8 weeks before the last frost date.

Start cauliflower 8 to 10 weeks before the last frost date.

Start annual flowers and herbs by seed indoors 8 to 12 weeks before last frost date.

Start basil, cilantro, and kale indoors 4 to 6 weeks before the last frost date.

Cut logs for spring mushroom inoculation.

Harvest sunchokes (Jerusalem artichokes) when the soil is workable.

Tap maple trees (high temps must be above freezing and low temps below freezing).

Harvest wild edibles.

Prune fruit trees before growth begins but after the coldest weather has passed.

Test your soil if you didn't in the fall. Add nutrients as necessary.

Turn compost once it's workable.

Watch damage from deer, mice, and voles on fruit trees and bushes. Erect fencing if necessary.

Prune summer-bearing raspberry plants by removing all canes that produced fruit. Leave 3 to 6 strong new canes per linear foot.

Prune everbearing raspberry plants for a summer and fall harvest by removing the portions of primocanes that produced fruit in the fall. Remove all canes that have fully fruited.

Prune everbearing raspberry plants only to 3 inches above the ground for a fall harvest.

Prune blueberry plants and apply at least 1 inch of mulch to smother any mummy berry fungus if applicable.

Lightly prune trailing blackberries to maintain their shape.

Plant bare-root fruit trees, berry bushes (including strawberries), and perennials if the ground is workable.

Spray bushes and fruit trees before the buds break for specific diseases or pests if necessary.

Direct-sow flower seeds for spring growing, such as arnica, calendula, chamomile, columbine, lupine, and marshmallow.

April

When your onion seedlings arrive in the mail, plant them in the garden. If you started them from seed, transplant them outside.

Transplant lettuce and spinach seedlings into the garden under a low tunnel or hoop house.

Transplant broccoli, Brussels sprouts, cabbage, and cauliflower into the garden.

Start cucumber seeds in a cold frame.

Plant potatoes in the garden.

Transplant pepper and tomato seedlings into bigger pots.

Start heat-tolerant lettuce (such as butterhead and romaine) indoors.

Start Swiss chard indoors 4 weeks before the last frost date.

Start marjoram and winter and summer squash seeds indoors 2 to 3 weeks before the last frost date.

Direct-sow beets, carrots, kale, lettuce, peas, potatoes, radishes, and turnips 2 to 4 weeks before the last frost.

Inoculate mushroom logs.

Harvest dandelion greens.

Forage wild mushrooms (such as morel).

Plant bare-root fruit trees and berry bushes (including strawberries) if you didn't in March.

Put out a rain gauge and record the readings in your garden planner.

Check routinely for insects and other pests in the garden.

Pull weeds.

Turn compost.

Apply compost around the base of fruit trees.

Harvest dandelion greens.

When fruit trees and bushes blossom, spray them for specific diseases or pests as necessary.

May

Start melon seeds indoors on the last frost date.

Start harvesting some of the small leaves on the early planted lettuce.

Start harvesting green onions.

Start more heat-tolerant lettuce outside in a covered location, such as a back porch.

Transplant celery seedlings into the garden.

Remove your cold frame and put it away until fall.

Transplant basil, marjoram, melon, okra, peppers, squash (summer and winter), and tomatoes into the garden 2 to 4 weeks after the last frost provided that nights are at least 55 degrees F.

Transplant Swiss chard into the garden.

Direct-sow cabbage, cauliflower, cilantro, and parsnips 2 weeks before the last frost date.

Direct-sow basil, beans, dill, and sweet potatoes 3 to 4 weeks after the last frost date.

Direct-sow corn 2 weeks after the last frost date.

Direct-sow marjoram and summer savory 1 week after the last frost date.

Direct-sow spinach 6 weeks before the last frost date.

Harvest dandelion flowers, lamb's-quarter, ramps, rhubarb, stinging nettles, and violets.

Plant bare-root fruit trees and bushes if you didn't in the fall.

Plant potted fruit trees and bushes after the threat of frost has passed.

Plant sweet potato slips.

Forage wild mushrooms (such as morel).

Check routinely for insects and other pests in the garden.

Pull weeds.

Turn compost.

Harvest young red raspberry plant leaves for tea before the plant begins to flower.

June

Harvest asparagus, peas, rhubarb, and strawberries.

At the end of June, pull out peas and replace them with beans.

Harvest beets, broccoli, carrots, lettuce, and spinach.

Cut back comfrey and use it as mulch or compost, or give to your chickens as fodder.

Harvest herbs.

Harvest purslane tips.

Check routinely for insects and other pests in the garden.

Pull weeds.

Turn compost.

Transplant potted bushes and fruit trees.

Cut to the ground any root suckers near fruit trees.

Place netting over bushes and fruit trees as the fruit ripens to prevent bird damage.

Cut off the tips of blackberry primocanes to increase the fruit yield.

Succession-sow beets, greens, lettuce, and radishes every 2 to 3 weeks for a continual summer harvest.

Harvest lavender buds before they bloom for teas and medicine.

Harvest herbal flower blossoms for tea and salves.

July

Start broccoli, cabbage, and cauliflower indoors for a fall garden 14 to 16 weeks before the first frost date.

If the tops of onions have fallen over, harvest and cure them.

If soft-neck garlic tops have fallen over, harvest and cure them. If the top 2 or 3 sets of leaves on hard-neck garlic have turned brown, harvest and cure them.

Pull up walking (Egyptian) onions. Clip the tops and allow the tops and bottoms to dry until October.

Harvest beans, broccoli, cabbage, cauliflower, cherries, cucumbers, early blueberries, peppers, raspberries, summer squash, and zucchini.

Cut back comfrey and use it as mulch or compost, or give it to your chickens as fodder.

Harvest herbs.

Harvest purslane tips.

Check routinely for insects and other pests in the garden.

Pull weeds.

Water.

Watch for powdery mildew.

Fertilize containers.

Turn compost.

Cut to the ground any root suckers near fruit trees.

Place netting over fruit trees as the fruit ripens to prevent bird damage.

Cut off the tips of blackberry primocanes to increase the fruit yield.

August

Transplant broccoli, cabbage, and cauliflower seedlings into a fall garden. Keep well-watered!

Direct-sow carrot seeds into a fall garden 8 to 12 weeks before the first frost date. Keep the seed bed shaded and well-watered.

Start fall lettuce seeds indoors.

Direct-sow beets and radishes 8 weeks before the first frost date.

Direct-sow broccoli, chard, parsnips, and peas 12 weeks before the first frost date.

Direct-sow Brussels sprouts 10 weeks before the first frost date.

Direct-sow cabbage, cilantro, kale, lettuce, and spinach 6 to 8 weeks before the first frost date.

Harvest apples, beans, blackberries, blueberries, corn, cucumbers, peaches, peppers, plums, raspberries, summer squash, and tomatoes.

Cut back comfrey and use it as mulch or compost, or give it to your chickens as fodder.

Harvest herbs.

Harvest purslane tips.

Harvest elderberries.

Check routinely for insects and other pests in the garden.

Pull weeds.

Water.

Watch for powdery mildew.

Fertilize containers.

Turn compost.

Place netting over fruit trees as the fruit ripens to prevent bird damage.

September

Transplant lettuce seedlings into the garden. Keep well-watered.

Direct-sow radishes and turnips 4 weeks before the first frost date.

Direct-sow garlic cloves 2 weeks before to 2 weeks after first frost date.

Harvest apples, beans, cabbage, grapes, pears, peppers, radishes, raspberries, summer squash, sweet potatoes, and tomatoes.

Harvest and cure winter squash.

Harvest nuts (butternut, chestnut, hazelnut, hickory, pecan, pine nut, and walnut).

Collect seeds from your garden herbs and plants.

Harvest herbs.

Harvest mushrooms on inoculated logs.

Harvest sunflowers for seeds.

Harvest dandelion roots.

Harvest purslane tips.

Harvest elderberries.

Harvest rose hips.

Forage wild mushrooms (such as chanterelle, chicken of the woods, lion's mane, lobster, oyster, and porcini).

Check routinely for insects and other pests in the garden. Treat for slugs because they come out in force during this month.

Pull weeds.

Water.

Clean up and remove any fallen fruit. Decaying fruit will harbor disease and pests.

Be prepared for frost.

Prune dead or diseased branches from nut trees.

ZONES 5–6

Turn compost.

Sow cover crops if using them.

October

Direct-sow garlic cloves 2 weeks before to 2 weeks after the first frost date.

Harvest apples, beans, Brussels sprouts, cabbage, celery, kale, lettuce, pears, pumpkins, parsnips, peppers, raspberries, and tomatoes.

Harvest nuts (butternut, chestnut, hazelnut, hickory, pecan, pine nut, and walnut).

Keep beets, carrots, lettuce, parsnips, spinach, and turnips covered with hoops to keep them growing.

Cut back asparagus ferns after the frost kill. Apply compost or manure, and mulch if necessary.

As heavy frost approaches, cover broccoli, Brussels sprouts, cabbage, and cauliflower to keep the plants actively growing until harvest.

Pull warm-weather crops that have been hit with frost.

Have your soil tested and amend it as necessary.

Pull weeds before prepping your garden beds for winter. Build up the soil by covering it with fallen leaves, compost, natural fertilizers (such as chicken manure), and so on.

Plant walking (Egyptian) onion tops that have been drying since July.

Plant bushes and fruit trees.

Collect seeds from garden herbs and plants.

Harvest sunflowers for seeds.

Harvest sunchokes (Jerusalem artichokes). Harvest only what you plan to use, because they do not cure and store well. Layer thickly with mulch to access longer.

Forage wild mushrooms (such as chanterelle, chicken of the woods, lion's mane, lobster, oyster, and porcini).

Harvest and cure winter squash.

Be prepared for frost.

Clean up and remove any fallen fruit. Decaying fruit will harbor disease and pests.

Prune nut trees of any dead or diseased branches.

Cut off the tips of blackberry primocanes to increase the fruit yield. For everbearing blackberry primocanes that have fruited, prune them back to the ground for a fall harvest only.

Drain your garden hoses and sprinklers and store them for winter.

Turn compost.

Spray bushes and fruit trees for specific diseases or pests if necessary.

Harvest echinacea root on 3-year-old or older plants after the first frost date.

Harvest dandelion roots before the ground freezes.

November

Have your soil tested and amend it as necessary. Build up the soil by covering it with fallen leaves, compost, natural fertilizers (such as chicken manure), and so on.

After the first hard freeze, cover garlic and walking (Egyptian) onions with a layer of shredded leaves or other mulch.

Start harvesting beets, broccoli, Brussels sprouts, cabbage, carrots, cauliflower, kale, parsnips, and turnips.

Cover root crops with a layer of shredded leaves or other mulch to help protect against deep freezes.

Turn compost one last time.

Drain your garden hoses and sprinklers and store them for winter if you haven't done that yet.

Watch for damage from deer, mice, and voles on fruit trees and bushes. If necessary, spray the plants for specific diseases or pests, and add fencing around them.

Direct-sow flower seeds for spring growing, such as arnica, calendula, chamomile, columbine, lupine, and marshmallow.

December

Finish harvesting carrots, lettuce, and other remaining crops.

Watch for damage from deer, mice, and voles on fruit trees and bushes, and add fencing around them if necessary.

ZONES 7-8

January

Plan out what crops you'll be growing this year (use the Crops for a Year worksheet on page 16). Take inventory of your seeds and order more if necessary.

Plan your garden layout, and use the Seed Starting and Planting chart on pages 18-20 to schedule your seed starting and transplanting.

Make sure all your tools are clean and sharp.

Start onions from seed indoors 10 to 12 weeks before the last frost date.

Start annual flowers and herbs by seed indoors 8 to 12 weeks before last frost date.

Prune summer-bearing raspberry plants by removing all canes that produced fruit. Leave 3 to 6 strong new canes per linear foot.

Prune everbearing raspberry plants for a summer and fall harvest by removing the portions of primocanes that produced fruit in the fall. Remove all canes that have fully fruited.

Prune everbearing raspberry plants for a fall harvest only to 3 inches above the ground.

February

Use cold stratification for any flowers or herbs seeds you'll be seed starting indoors, such as feverfew, horehound, hyssop, lavender, marshmallow, and yarrow.

Put together a cold frame and place it in your garden where you will grow warm-weather crops.

Tap maple trees (high temps must be above freezing and low temps below freezing).

Start cauliflower 8 to 10 weeks before the last frost date.

Start eggplant, summer savory, and tomatoes indoors 6 to 8 weeks before the last frost date.

Start peas indoors 8 weeks before the last frost.

Start broccoli, cabbage, lettuce, okra, spinach, and summer savory 6 weeks before the last frost date.

Start pepper seeds indoors 4 to 8 weeks before the last frost date.

Plant berry bushes (including strawberries), bare-root fruit trees, and perennials if the ground is workable.

Prune summer-bearing raspberry plants by removing all canes that produced fruit. Leave 3 to 6 strong new canes per linear foot.

Prune everbearing raspberry plants for a summer and fall harvest by removing the portions of primocanes that produced fruit in the fall. Remove all canes that have fully fruited.

Prune everbearing raspberry plants for a fall harvest only to 3 inches above the ground.

Prune blueberry plants and apply at least 1 inch of mulch to smother any mummy berry fungus if applicable.

Spray fruit trees and bushes before the buds break

for specific diseases or pests if necessary.

Direct-sow flower seeds for spring growing, such as arnica, calendula, chamomile, columbine, lupine, and marshmallow.

March

Start peppers and tomatoes indoors 8 to 10 weeks before the last frost.

Direct-sow onion bulbs and spinach 6 weeks before the last frost.

Start basil, cilantro, and kale indoors 4 to 6 weeks before the last frost date.

Start chard indoors 4 weeks before the last frost date.

Start Brussels sprouts, marjoram, and winter and summer squash seeds indoors 2 to 3 weeks before the last frost date.

Transplant cauliflower, lettuce, pea, and spinach seedlings into the garden 4 weeks before the last frost date.

Transplant onion sets into the garden 2 to 4 weeks before the last frost date.

Direct-sow beets, carrots, kale, lettuce, peas, potatoes, radishes, and turnips 2 to 4 weeks before the last frost.

Prune any fruit bushes or trees you didn't prune in February.

Prune summer-bearing raspberry plants by removing all canes that produced fruit. Leave 3 to 6 strong new canes per linear foot.

Prune everbearing raspberry plants for a summer and fall harvest by removing the portions of primocanes that produced fruit in the fall. Remove all canes that have fully fruited.

Prune everbearing raspberry plants for a fall harvest only to 3 inches above the ground.

Prune blueberry plants and apply at least 1 inch of mulch to smother any mummy berry fungus if necessary.

Plant bare-root fruit trees, berry bushes (including strawberries), and perennials if you didn't in February.

Lightly prune trailing blackberries to maintain their shape.

Plant or divide and transplant perennials, such as asparagus and rhubarb.

Prune perennial herbs (such as lavender and rosemary) to retain their shape, size, and health as needed.

April

Transplant lettuce and spinach seedlings into the garden under a low tunnel or hoop house.

Transplant broccoli, cabbage, and kale seedlings into the garden 2 weeks before the last frost date.

Put out a rain gauge and record the readings in your garden planner.

Direct-sow cabbage, cauliflower, cilantro, and parsnips 2 weeks before the last frost date.

Start melon seeds indoors on the last frost date.

Transplant beets, chard, and cilantro into the garden on the last frost date.

Begin harvesting young stinging nettle leaves while they are still young and before the flowers head, ideally before they are a foot tall and the top has 2 or 3 sets of leaves. Wear gloves!

Harvest dandelion flowers, lamb's-quarter, ramps, and violets.

Spray fruit trees and bushes at blossom time for specific diseases or pests if necessary.

Apply compost around the base of fruit trees.

Pull weeds.

Turn compost.

Forage wild mushrooms (such as morel).

May

Transplant Brussels sprout seedlings into the garden 2 weeks after the last frost date.

Transplant basil, all herbal flowers, marjoram, melon, okra, pepper, squash (summer and winter), and tomato seedlings into the garden 3 to 4 weeks after the last frost, provided that nights are at least 55 degrees F.

Direct-sow marjoram and summer savory 1 week after the last frost date.

Direct-sow corn 2 weeks after the last frost date.

Direct-sow basil, beans, dill, and sweet potatoes 3 to 4 weeks after the last frost date.

Harvest dandelion flowers, lamb's-quarter, ramps, rhubarb, stinging nettles, and violets.

Harvest young red raspberry leaves for tea before the plant begins to flower.

Inoculate mushroom logs.

Pull weeds.

Turn compost.

June

Harvest asparagus, peas, rhubarb, and strawberries.

Start broccoli indoors for a fall garden 14 to 16 weeks before the first frost date.

Succession-sow beans, greens, lettuce, and radishes every 2 to 3 weeks for continual summer harvest.

Apply netting to fruit bushes and trees as needed to protect from birds, deer, and other pests.

Cut back comfrey and use it as mulch or compost, or give it to your chickens as fodder.

Check routinely for insects and other pests in the garden.

Pull weeds.

Turn compost.

Cut to the ground any root suckers near fruit trees.

Harvest lavender buds before they bloom for teas and medicine.

Harvest herbal flower blossoms for tea and salves.

July

Start Brussels sprouts and cabbage indoors.

Start cauliflower indoors for a fall garden 12 to 14 weeks before the first frost date.

Transplant broccoli starts into the garden 10 to 12 weeks before the first frost date.

Direct-sow broccoli, chard, parsnips, and peas for a fall harvest 12 weeks before the first frost date.

Direct-sow Brussels sprouts 10 weeks before the first frost in fall.

Harvest beans, early blueberries, broccoli, cabbage, cauliflower, cherries, cucumbers, peppers, raspberries, summer squash, and zucchini.

If the tops of onions have fallen over, harvest and cure them.

If soft-neck garlic tops have fallen over, harvest and cure them. If the top 2 or 3 sets of leaves on hard-neck garlic have turned brown, harvest and cure them.

Pull up walking (Egyptian) onions, clip the tops, and allow the tops and bottoms to dry until October.

Harvest herbal flower blossoms for tea and salves.

Harvest purslane tips.

Check routinely for insects and other pests in the garden.

Pull weeds.

Water.

ZONES 7–8

217

Watch for powdery mildew.

Fertilize containers.

Turn compost.

Cut to the ground any root suckers near trees.

Place netting over bushes and fruit trees as the fruit ripens to prevent bird damage.

Cut off the tips of blackberry primocanes to increase the fruit yield.

August

Transplant cauliflower starts into a fall garden 8 weeks before the first frost date.

Direct-sow carrots 8 to 12 weeks before the first frost date.

Direct-sow beets and radishes 8 weeks before the first frost date.

Direct-sow cabbage, cilantro, kale, lettuce, and spinach 6 to 8 weeks before the first frost date.

Purchase seed garlic if needed.

Sow cover crops if you are using them for fall and winter.

Harvest apples, apricots, beans, blackberries, blueberries, corn, cucumbers, peaches, peppers, plums, raspberries, summer squash, and tomatoes.

Harvest and cure winter squash that's ready.

Cut back comfrey and use it as mulch or compost, or give it to your chickens as fodder.

Harvest herbs.

Harvest purslane tips.

Harvest elderberries.

Check routinely for insects and other garden pests.

Pull weeds.

Water.

Watch for powdery mildew.

Fertilize containers.

Turn compost.

Place netting over fruit trees as the fruit ripens to prevent bird damage.

September

Harvest apples, beans, cabbage, grapes, pears, radishes, raspberries, peppers, summer squash, sweet potatoes, and tomatoes.

Harvest and cure winter squash.

Harvest nuts (butternut, chestnut, hazelnut, hickory, pine nut, pecan, and walnut).

Collect seeds from garden herbs and plants.

Harvest herbs.

Harvest mushrooms on inoculated logs.

Harvest sunflowers for seeds.

Harvest dandelion roots.

Harvest purslane tips.

Harvest elderberries.

Harvest rose hips.

Forage wild mushrooms (such as chanterelle, chicken of the woods, lion's mane, lobster, oyster, and porcini).

Check routinely for insects and other pests in the

garden. Treat for slugs, because they come out in force during this month.

Pull weeds.

Water.

Clean up and remove any fallen fruit. Decaying fruit will harbor disease and pests.

Be prepared for frost.

Prune dead or diseased branches from nut trees.

Turn compost.

Start a new compost pile with fall leaves and grass clippings.

October

Plant garlic bulbs.

Watch for the first frost warning, and use crop extenders on warm-weather crops to extend the season if desired.

Cover beets, carrots, lettuce, parsnips, spinach, and turnips with hoops to keep them growing.

Start harvesting larger beets, carrots, parsnips, and turnips. Cover them with a layer of shredded leaves or other mulch.

As heavy frost approaches, cover broccoli, Brussels sprouts, cabbage, and cauliflower to keep the plants actively growing until harvest.

Apply compost or manure to perennial plants. If you're using sheet compost or mulch, apply it to your garden beds to protect the soil over the winter.

Apply straw or mulch to any plants that need protection from winter temps.

Cut back asparagus ferns after the frost kill. Apply compost or manure and mulch if needed.

Transplant fruit bushes and trees if necessary. If winters are mild, you can plant fruit trees in fall, but if a cold or extreme winter is predicted, wait for spring.

Direct-sow annual and perennial flower seeds for your zone for next spring.

Have your soil tested and amend it as necessary.

Pull weeds before prepping your garden beds for winter. Build up the soil by covering it with fallen leaves, compost, natural fertilizers such as chicken manure, and so on.

Plant walking (Egyptian) onion tops that have been drying since July.

Plant fruit trees and bushes.

Collect seeds from garden herbs and plants.

Harvest sunflowers for seeds.

Harvest sunchokes (Jerusalem artichokes). Harvest only what you plan to use because they do not cure and store well. Add a thick layer of mulch to keep them healthy.

Start harvesting beets, broccoli, Brussels sprouts, cabbage, carrots, cauliflower, kale, parsnips, and turnips.

Cover root crops with a layer of shredded leaves or other mulch to help protect against deep freezes.

Forage wild mushrooms (such as chanterelle, chicken of the woods, lion's mane, lobster, oyster, and porcini).

Harvest and cure winter squash.

Be prepared for frost.

Clean up and remove any fallen fruit. Decaying fruit will harbor disease and pests.

Prune nut trees of any dead or diseased branches.

Cut off the tips of blackberry primocanes to increase the fruit yield. For everbearing blackberry primocanes that have fruited, prune them back to the ground for a fall harvest only.

Drain your garden hoses and sprinklers and store them for the winter.

Turn compost.

Spray fruit trees and bushes for specific diseases or pests if necessary.

Harvest echinacea root on 3-year-old or older plants after the first frost date.

Harvest dandelion roots before the ground freezes.

November

After the first hard freeze, cover garlic and walking (Egyptian) onions with a layer of shredded leaves or other mulch.

Continue harvesting beets, broccoli, Brussels sprouts, cabbage, carrots, cauliflower, kale, parsnips, and turnips.

Cover root crops with a layer of shredded leaves or other mulch to help protect against deep freezes.

Turn compost one last time.

Drain your garden hoses and sprinklers and store them for the winter if you haven't done that yet.

Direct-sow flower seeds for spring growing, such as arnica, calendula, chamomile, columbine, lupine, and marshmallow.

Spray fruit trees and bushes for specific diseases or pests if necessary.

December

Finish harvesting Brussels sprouts and remaining .cool-weather crops.

ZONES 9–10+

January

Plan out what crops you'll be growing this year (use the Crops for a Year worksheet on page 16). Take inventory of your seeds and order more if necessary.

Plan your garden layout, and use the Seed Starting and Planting chart on pages 18-20 to schedule your seed starting and transplanting.

Make sure all your tools are clean and sharp.

Mix compost into your garden and add mulch.

Plant or sow beets, broccoli, cabbage, carrots, cauliflower, celery, lettuce, spinach, onions, peas, and potatoes.

Sow cilantro.

Harvest broccoli, carrots, cauliflower, and greens.

Prep garden beds for spring planting.

Start seeds late in the month.

Harvest grapefruit, lemons, limes, oranges, and starfruit.

Plant blackberries, blueberries, and raspberries (check varieties for zone specificity).

February

Mix in compost before planting and add mulch.

Plant onion sets in the garden.

Plant or sow beets, carrots, celery, collards, lettuce, mustard, green onions, peas, potatoes, and radishes.

If you're starting seeds, do it now.

Sow cilantro.

Harvest strawberries.

Harvest starfruit.

Harvest chickweed, dandelion greens, and plantain while young.

March

Mix in compost before planting and add mulch.

Plant or sow beans, beets, carrots, collards, lettuce, melons, mustard, green onions, peas, radishes, summer squash, and tomatoes.

Harvest strawberries.

Plant muscadine grapes and kiwi.

April

Mix in compost before planting and add mulch.

Plant or sow okra, sweet potatoes, and winter squash. Clean out beds of winter crops that have most likely bolted by now.

May

Water.

Pull weeds.

Harvest beans, summer squash, and tomatoes.

Harvest herbs.

Mulch garden.

Harvest blackberries and mango.

Harvest lavender buds before they bloom for teas and medicine.

June

Water.

Pull weeds.

Continue harvesting beans, summer squash, and tomatoes.

Check routinely for insects and other pests in the garden.

Mulch the garden.

Harvest blackberries, mango, and starfruit.

Harvest herbs.

Harvest garlic.

Apply netting to fruit bushes and trees as needed to protect from birds, deer, and other pests.

July

Mix in compost before planting.

Plant peppers and tomatoes.

Water a lot.

Pull weeds.

Continue harvesting beans, summer squash, and tomatoes. Melons should be ripening.

Consider using shade cloth to cover some plants to avoid sun scorch. Tomatoes are prone to this.

Winter squash will be ready by end of month.

Harvest onions.

Clean out garden areas and add mulch.

Plant fruit trees (avocado, banana, citrus—orange, lemon, lime, grapefruit—fig, jackfruit, loquat, lychee, olives, persimmon, pomegranate, and starfruit). In zones 10 and warmer, plant mango and papaya.

Harvest figs, mangoes, pomegranate, and starfruit.

Harvest herbs.

August

Water a lot.

Pull weeds.

Harvest okra and peppers. Summer squash and tomatoes might be ready, but the heat will cause them to struggle. Consider pulling the weaker plants.

Plan fall garden.

Plant fruit trees (avocado, banana, citrus—orange, lemon, lime, grapefruit—fig, jackfruit, loquat, lychee, olives, persimmon, pomegranate, and starfruit). In zones 10 and warmer, plant mango and papaya.

Harvest figs, mangoes, muscadine grapes, persimmons, pomegranates, and starfruit.

Forage wild mushrooms.

Harvest herbs.

September

Water.

Pull weeds.

Harvest okra, peppers, and sweet potatoes.

Mix in compost before planting.

Plant or sow beans, cabbage, corn, cucumbers, eggplant, kale, lettuce, mustard, onions, peas, peppers, pumpkins, radishes, summer squash, tomatoes, and turnips.

Plant cilantro.

Harvest figs, kiwis, muscadine grapes, nuts, persimmons, pomegranates, and starfruit.

Forage wild mushrooms.

Harvest herbs.

October

Water.

Pull weeds.

Mix in compost before planting.

Plant or sow a fall garden: beets, broccoli, cabbage, carrots, cauliflower, celery, collards, kale, lettuce, mustard, onions, peas, radishes, spinach, strawberries, turnips, Swiss chard, kohlrabi, summer squash, and zucchini.

Plant potatoes in mid to northern regions of zone 9.

Plant fruit trees (avocado, banana, citrus—orange, lemon, lime, grapefruit—fig, jackfruit, loquat, lychee, persimmon, and pomegranate). Plant mango and papaya in zones 10 and warmer.

Plant nut trees (chestnut, pecan).

Harvest figs, kiwis, nuts, persimmons, pomegranates, and starfruits.

Harvest herbs.

Direct-sow cover crops if using them for fall or winter.

November

Harvest lettuce and other greens.

Mix in compost before planting.

Plant or sow beets, broccoli, Brussels sprouts, cabbage, carrots, cauliflower, celery, collards, kale, kohlrabi, lettuce, mustard, onions, peas, radishes, spinach, strawberries, Swiss chard, and turnips. Plant garlic in zone 9.

Cover tomatoes if temps go below freezing. You don't need to cover anything else unless temps are in the low twenties.

Plant parsley.

Harvest kiwi, nuts, persimmon, pomegranate, and starfruit.

Plant nut trees (chestnut, pecan).

Harvest herbs.

Plant blueberries and raspberries (check varieties for zone specificity).

December

Use cold stratification for any flowers or herbs seeds you'll be seed starting indoors, such as feverfew, horehound, hyssop, lavender, marshmallow, and yarrow.

Harvest broccoli, cauliflower, and greens.

Mix in compost before planting.

Plant or sow beets, broccoli, Brussels sprouts, cabbage, carrots, cauliflower, celery, collards, kale, lettuce, mustard, onions, peas, radishes, and Swiss chard. Plant garlic in zone 9.

Plant parsley.

Harvest starfruit.

Plant blackberries and day-neutral strawberries (check varieties for zone specificity).

Plant nut trees (chestnut, pecan).

Harvest dandelion and echinacea root before the ground freezes.